Hajj Book

The Farewell Hajj *of* Rasulullah Sallallahu 'Alaihi Wasallam

Hajjatul Wadaa'

Published By:
Islamic Book Store

Hajj Book

Hajjatul Wadaa'

The Farewell Hajj of Rasulullah

(sallallahu 'alaihi wasallam)

A humble appeal is made to the readers to offer suggestions, corrections, etc. to improve the quality of this publication in the future. May Allah Ta'ala reward you for this.

The writers, editors and typesetters humbly request your du'aas for them, their parents, families, Asaatizah and Mashaayikh.

Prepared by:

Ibnu Mas'ood Institute & Uswatul Muslimah

4 Third Avenue
P.O. Box 26024
Isipingo Beach
4115
South Africa

Tel:	+27 31 902 9818 (ext. 6)
WhatsApp:	+27 72 566 4856
Telegram:	t.me/imi_um
E-mail:	info@ibnumasood.co.za / info@uswatulmuslimah.co.za
First Edition:	Zul Hijjah 1444 / June 2023

Published by:

Islamic Book Store
Gujarat (India)
394601

Contents

Introduction 1
Departure From Madeenah Munawwarah 6
    Number of Sahaabah (radhiyallahu 'anhum) 6
    Wives and Niqaab 7
    Date of Departure 8
    Khutbah 8
Zul Hulaifah – First Stop 9
    Jibreel ('alaihis salaam) 9
    Ghusl 10
    Camels 10
    Ihraam and Perfume 11
    Types of Hajj 11
    Talbiyah 11
    Humility and Sincerity 13
    Asmaa bintu 'Umais (radhiyallahu 'anha) 14
    Talbiyah Aloud 14
    Cupping at Malal 15
Other Stops 16
    Rowhaa – Second Stop 16

Ithaabah – Third Stop 17

'Arj – Fourth Stop 17

Abwaa' – Fifth Stop 19

'Usfaan – Sixth Stop 19

Sarif – Seventh Stop 20

Zu Tuwaa – Eight Stop 22

Incidents Enroute 23

Anjashah (radhiyallahu 'anhu) 23

Camel of Safiyyah (radhiyallahu 'anha) 25

Makkah Mukarramah 27

Ghusl 27

Moosa ('alaihis salaam) 27

Entering 28

Tawaaf 28

Two Rakaats and Zamzam 29

Sa'ee 30

Love and Obedience 32

Abtah 34

Arrival of 'Ali (radhiyallahu 'anhu) 34

Visiting Sa'd (radhiyallahu 'anhu) 36

Mina 37

Proceeding to Mina 37

Tying Ihraam 37
Five Salaahs 37

'Arafaat

Leaving Mina 39
Breaking the Custom of the Quraish 39
Historic Khutbah 40
Sanctity of a Muslim 41
Aspects of Ignorance 41
Treatment of Wives 44
Right of Husbands 45
Rights of Wives 46
Book of Allah 47
Conveyed the Message 47
Not Fasting 48
Joining Zuhr and 'Asr 48
Wuqoof and Du'aa 49
Perfection of Deen 52
Boasting about the Sahaabah (radhiyallahu 'anhum) 54

Muzdalifah

Departure from 'Arafaat 55
Traveling with Calmness 55
Dismounting 56
Joining Salaahs and Sleeping 56

Women and Children 57

Pebbles and Wuqoof 57

Acceptance of Du'aa 58

10th Zul Hijjah 60

Departure from Muzdalifah 60

Batnu Muhassir 60

Pelting 62

Farewell Hajj 62

Farewell Khutbah 63

Time has Rotated 63

Sanctity of a Muslim 65

Meeting Allah Ta'ala 67

Internal Fighting 67

Passing the Message 67

Importance of Segregation 68

Allocating Places 69

Slaughtering the Camels 69

Partaking of the Meat 71

Blessed Hair 71

Going to Makkah Mukarramah 72

Remaining Days 74

Pelting 74

Surah Nasr 74

Khutbah	75
Oppression and Extortion	75
Internal Fighting	77
Racism	78
Fulfilling the Trust	79
Insignificant Sins	80
True Muslim, Mu-min, Muhaajir and Mujaahid	81
Departure from Mina	82
Muhassab	83
Final Tawaaf and Fajr	83
'Umrah of Aaishah (radhiyallahu 'anha)	83

Return 85

Departure	85
Ghadeeru Khum	85
Night in Zul Hulaifah	85
Uhud	86
Du'aa	86
Like Hajj with Me	87

بِسْمِ اللهِ الرَّحْمٰنِ الرَّحِيْمِ

اَللّٰهُمَّ صَلِّ عَلٰى سَيِّدِنَا وَحَبِيْبِنَا وَمَوْلَانَا مُحَمَّدٍ وَّعَلٰى اٰلِ سَيِّدِنَا وَحَبِيْبِنَا وَمَوْلَانَا مُحَمَّدٍ وَّأَصْحَابِهٖ وَأَزْوَاجِهٖ وَأَوْلَادِهٖ وَأَهْلِ بَيْتِهٖ وَذُرِّيَّتِهٖ وَمُحِبِّيْهِ وَأَتْبَاعِهٖ وَأَشْيَاعِهٖ وَعَلَيْنَا مَعَهُمْ اَجْمَعِيْنَ يَا اَرْحَمَ الرَّاحِمِيْنَ

Introduction

Rasulullah (sallallahu 'alaihi wasallam) only performed one hajj after hajj was made fardh on the Ummah. This hajj was performed in the tenth year after hijrah and is famously known as "Hajjatul Wadaa' - The Farewell Pilgrimage".

The reason for this hajj being referred to as the "Farewell Pilgrimage" is that Rasulullah (sallallahu 'alaihi wasallam) left this world just eighty-one days after the day of 'Arafah. Hence, this hajj was performed slightly less than three months before his demise. *(Tafseer Ibni Katheer vol. 3, pg. 315)*

Furthermore, Rasulullah (sallallahu 'alaihi wasallam) bade the Sahaabah (radhiyallahu 'anhum) farewell and delivered his

parting advices to the Ummah during this hajj. *(Saheeh Bukhaari #1739 & #1742)* Rasulullah (sallallahu 'alaihi wasallam) had said to them,

« خُذُوْا عَنِّيْ مَنَاسِكَكُمْ ، لَعَلِّيْ لَا أَرَاكُمْ بَعْدَ عَامِيْ هٰذَا »

""Learn the rites of hajj from me, perhaps I will not see you after this year." (Sunan Tirmizi #886 and As-Sunanul Kubraa – Baihaqi #9524)

On account of these reasons, the Sahaabah (radhiyallahu 'anhum) would call this hajj "Hajjatul Wadaa'", even during the lifetime of Rasulullah (sallallahu 'alaihi wasallam). *(Saheeh Bukhaari #4402)*

The great 'Aalim and historian of recent times, Moulana Sayyid Abul Hasan 'Ali Nadwi (rahimahullah), has very beautifully and accurately described this hajj of Rasulullah (sallallahu 'alaihi wasallam).

He explains that the hajj of Rasulullah (sallallahu 'alaihi wasallam) was miraculous and unique in various respects. It stood out for many different reasons, such as the manner in which Rasulullah (sallallahu 'alaihi wasallam) imparted 'ilm and propagated Deen during this hajj and the manner in which he attended to and supervised the Deeni progress of the Sahaabah (radhiyallahu 'anhum), even correcting them if necessary. Similarly, the spiritual dimension of his (sallallahu 'alaihi wasallam) hajj was unique.

The Sahaabah (radhiyallahu 'anhum) were aflame with the love of Rasulullah (sallallahu 'alaihi wasallam). Hence, when he announced that he was departing for hajj, they flocked to him from every area, like moths attracted to a candle-flame, and remained attached to him from the beginning until the end of this blessed journey.

Perhaps one of the most outstanding and unparalleled aspects of the Final Hajj is the manner in which the Sahaabah (radhiyallahu 'anhum) ensured that they recorded every minute detail of this journey, from the time Rasulullah (sallallahu 'alaihi wasallam) departed from Madeenah Munawwarah until he arrived in Makkah Mukarramah, throughout the days of hajj, and until he again returned to Madeenah Munawwarah.

On account of their consuming love for Rasulullah (sallallahu 'alaihi wasallam), they even recorded the seemingly mundane details such as the place, the limb and the day on which Rasulullah (sallallahu 'alaihi wasallam) underwent cupping during this blessed journey and the 'itr (perfume) that he applied, the limbs on which it was applied, and who had applied it.

Their devotion to the Master (sallallahu 'alaihi wasallam), was such that they recorded his hajj and other similar events with such detail that these occasions remain preserved until Qiyaamah, and the one reading them can literally visualize the events unfolding before his eyes.

There was great wisdom in Allah Ta'ala allowing the details of this hajj to be preserved and in Him deciding that the hajj would occur at the very end of the life of Rasulullah (sallallahu 'alaihi wasallam). Islam had spread far and wide, the Muslims were many in number and Islam was now strong and on the increase. The hearts of the Sahaabah (radhiyallahu 'anhum) were ever-thirsty to receive even more guidance from Rasulullah (sallallahu 'alaihi wasallam), and it was nearly time for him (sallallahu 'alaihi wasallam) to depart from this world. Hence, this hajj would serve as a farewell to the Ummah, in which Rasulullah (sallallahu 'alaihi wasallam) would deliver his parting advices and teach them their Deen and hajj.

Therefore, this hajj equated a thousand lectures and a thousand lessons, as it was a moving classroom in which those who were unlearned were able to learn, those who were ignorant were educated and all were spiritually charged on account of the blessed company and presence of Rasulullah (sallallahu 'alaihi wasallam). *(Summarised and adapted from Hajjatul Wadaa' pgs. 46-49)*

This booklet is a humble effort to present the details of this amazing hajj journey of Rasulullah (sallallahu 'alaihi wasallam), together with the various pertinent parting advices that he offered to His Ummah.

Explaining the importance of these advices, the great Muhaddith, Moulana Habeebur Rahmaan Aa'zami (rahimahullah) writes, "Due to the sermons of Rasulullah (sallallahu 'alaihi wasallam) during his hajj being so great, and due to them comprising of important matters and beneficial advices, it is imperative for every Muslim to keep them before him (at all times). Similarly, it is essential for every person performing hajj to remind himself of these advices when he is standing at those (blessed) places which are overflowing with noor (divine light) and blessings. *(Juz-u Khutubaatin Nabi [sallallahu 'alaihi wasallam])*

Although most of the references have been provided, wherever a reference has not been given, that content has been taken from the book, "Hajjatul Wadaa'", written by Shaikhul Hadeeth Moulana Muhammad Zakariyya Kandhelwi (rahimahullah).

May Allah Ta'ala accept this humble effort and make it a means of us being blessed with the true love and obedience of Rasulullah (sallallahu 'alaihi wasallam), and with his noble company on the Day of Qiyaamah and in Jannah, aameen.

لَبَّيْكَ اَللّٰهُمَّ لَبَّيْكَ ، لَبَّيْكَ لَا شَرِيْكَ لَكَ لَبَّيْكَ ، إِنَّ الْحَمْدَ وَالنِّعْمَةَ لَكَ وَالْمُلْكَ ، لَا شَرِيْكَ لَكَ

Departure From Madeenah Munawwarah

Number of Sahaabah (radhiyallahu 'anhum)

When Rasulullah (sallallahu 'alaihi wasallam) announced to the Sahaabah (radhiyallahu 'anhum) that he intended performing hajj, the Sahaabah (radhiyallahu 'anhum) of Madeenah Munawwarah and the surrounding areas immediately prepared to join him and perform hajj with him.

Such was their enthusiasm to join Rasulullah (sallallahu 'alaihi wasallam) that even if they lacked a conveyance, they were not deterred. Instead, they set out on foot and completed the journey walking. *(Sunan Nasai #2761)*

The Sahaabah (radhiyallahu 'anhum) who accompanied Rasulullah (sallallahu 'alaihi wasallam) for the farewell hajj were more than one hundred thousand in number, and the group they formed was so large that it extended as far as the eye could see. *(Saheeh Muslim #1218 and Awjazul Masaalik vol. 6, pg. 510)*

Wives and Niqaab

When departing on the journey of hajj, Rasulullah (sallallahu 'alaihi wasallam) also took all his respected wives with him. His respected wives were seated in a hawdaj, as was the norm among the Arabs at that time for women who were traveling. *(Tabaqaat Ibni Sa'd vol. 2, pg. 173)*

A hawdaj is a canopy that was roofed and would be tied to the back of the camel. *(Hadyus Saari pg. 323)* Women would sit in this canopy when traveling, and in this manner, they would remain sheltered and concealed from the gazes of strange men.

We should ponder and reflect that on the one hand, these were the blessed wives of Rasulullah (sallallahu 'alaihi wasallam), who were the purest of all women. On the other hand, the men present were Sahaabah (radhiyallahu 'anhum), the purest of men. Furthermore, they were travelling in the presence of Rasulullah (sallallahu 'alaihi wasallam). Yet, despite the piety and of their hearts, and the purity of their environment, they still ensured that the laws of hijaab and niqaab were upheld.

In comparison, we can well imagine how much more necessary it is for us to maintain the laws of hijaab and niqaab in this day and age, when our environment is charged with temptation and sin!

In another narration, our beloved mother, Sayyidah 'Aaishah (radhiyallahu 'anha) explained the emphasis they laid on covering their faces, even in the state of ihraam, in the following words: "Riders would pass by us while we (the womenfolk of

Rasulullah [sallallahu 'alaihi wasallam]) were with him in the state of ihraam. When they would come in line with us, we would lower our jilbaab from our heads to cover our faces (without allowing it to touch the face), and when they would pass, we would raise it." *(Sunan Abi Dawood #1833)*

Date of Departure

Rasulullah (sallallahu 'alaihi wasallam) departed from Madeenah Munawwarah on Saturday 25th Zul Qa'dah. That year, the month of Zul Qa'dah consisted of twenty-nine days.

Khutbah

Before departing, Rasulullah (sallallahu 'alaihi wasallam) delivered a khutbah to the Sahaabah (radhiyallahu 'anhum) and thereafter performed the Zuhr Salaah.

In this khutbah, he taught them the laws of ihraam. Rasulullah (sallallahu 'alaihi wasallam) then put on his sandals, applied oil to his blessed hair, wore his shawl and departed.

لَبَّيْكَ اَللّٰهُمَّ لَبَّيْكَ ، لَبَّيْكَ لَا شَرِيْكَ لَكَ لَبَّيْكَ ، إِنَّ الْحَمْدَ وَالنِّعْمَةَ لَكَ وَالْمُلْكَ ، لَا شَرِيْكَ لَكَ

Zul Hulaifah – First Stop

After departing, Rasulullah (sallallahu 'alaihi wasallam) made his first stop in Zul Hulaifah. Zul Hulaifah is a place approximately nine kilometres from Madeenah Munawwarah in which the blessed valley of 'Aqeeq is found.

Rasulullah (sallallahu 'alaihi wasallam) performed 'Asr Salaah in Zul Hulaifah as a musaafir (two rakaats), and also spent the night there.

Rasulullah (sallallahu 'alaihi wasallam) only left Zul Hulaifah after the Zuhr Salaah of the next day. Hence, he performed five salaahs in Zul Hulaifah.

Jibreel ('alaihis salaam)

During that night, while Rasulullah (sallallahu 'alaihi wasallam) was in Zul Hulaifah, Allah Ta'ala sent Jibreel ('alaihis salaam) to him with the following instruction:

«صَلِّ فِيْ هٰذَا الْوَادِي الْمُبَارَكِ ، وَقُلْ عُمْرَةٌ فِيْ حَجَّةٍ»

"Perform salaah in this blessed valley (of 'Aqeeq) and say 'an 'umrah in a hajj' (i.e. make the intention of performing the qiraan hajj, in which

'umrah and hajj are performed with one ihraam)." (Saheeh Bukhaari #1534 and Fat-hul Baari)

Ghusl

That night, Rasulullah (sallallahu 'alaihi wasallam) shared the bed with all his respected wives. In the early morning, Rasulullah (sallallahu 'alaihi wasallam) performed ghusl for janaabah.

Later during that day, Rasulullah (sallallahu 'alaihi wasallam) performed another ghusl for entering into ihraam.

Camels

Rasulullah (sallallahu 'alaihi wasallam) had brought many camels with him as Hady (sacrificial animals). These camels of Rasulullah (sallallahu 'alaihi wasallam) were in the care of Sayyiduna Naajiyah Aslami (radhiyallahu 'anhu).

Before entering the state of ihraam, Rasulullah (sallallahu 'alaihi wasallam) hung sandals around the necks of these camels and also pierced their sides slightly, causing a little blood to flow. Thereafter, the blood was smeared on their humps.[1]

---

[1] Hanging sandals around the camels' necks and smearing blood on their humps was a common practice at that time in order to mark them as sacrificial camels of hajj so that the disbelievers would not interfere with them.

Ihraam and Perfume

After performing a second ghusl, Rasulullah (sallallahu 'alaihi wasallam) wore his lungi and shawl (the upper and lower garments of ihraam).

Using her own hands, Sayyidah 'Aaishah (radhiyallahu 'anha) applied an 'itr (perfume) known as 'zareerah' and another 'itr containing musk to the blessed head and body of Rasulullah (sallallahu 'alaihi wasallam).

Rasulullah (sallallahu 'alaihi wasallam) also applied 'ghisl' to his blessed hair. Ghisl refers to a substance that would be applied to the hair to keep it neat and prevent it from becoming dishevelled.

Types of Hajj

Rasulullah (sallallahu 'alaihi wasallam) explained the different types of hajj to the Sahaabah (radhiyallahu 'anhu) and gave them the choice of tying ihraam for hajj only (i.e. ifraad hajj), 'umrah (before hajj with separate ihraams i.e. tamattu' hajj) or both, hajj and 'umrah (with one ihraam for both i.e. qiraan hajj).

Talbiyah

Rasulullah (sallallahu 'alaihi wasallam) performed the two rakaats of Sunnatul Ihraam and then immediately recited the talbiyah for both hajj and 'umrah.

Accordingly, Rasulullah (sallallahu 'alaihi wasallam) was performing the qiraan hajj.

He thereafter mounted his she-camel, named Qaswaa[2], and recited the talbiyah again. When the camel ascended from the valley and reached Baydaa (an open field), Rasulullah (sallallahu 'alaihi wasallam) recited the talbiyah again.

On account of the large crowd of Sahaabah (radhiyallahu 'anhum), all the Sahaabah (radhiyallahu 'anhum) were unable to be with Rasulullah (sallallahu 'alaihi wasallam) all the time. Hence, some Sahaabah (radhiyallahu 'anhum) heard the first talbiyah, some heard the second, and some heard the third.

On hearing the talbiyah, each Sahaabi (radhiyallahu 'anhu) thought that Rasulullah (sallallahu 'alaihi wasallam) had only entered into ihraam at the place where he heard the talbiyah. Hence, he narrated accordingly.

It is for this reason that there is a difference in the ahaadeeth regarding the place where Rasulullah (sallallahu 'alaihi wasallam) entered into ihraam. This explanation has been given by Sayyiduna 'Abdullah bin 'Abbaas (radhiyallahu 'anhuma). (*Sunan Abi Dawood #1770*)

From this example, we can see that if a person has to try to practice on the hadeeth directly, he will fall into confusion, as in this case, the ahaadeeth all seem to contradict one another.

---

[2] This was the most famous camel of Raslulullah (sallallahu 'alaihi wasallam). It was also known as Adhbaa, Jad'aa and Kharmaa.

Hence, without the guidance of the Fuqahaa (jurists), a person will not be able to practice on Deen correctly.

Humility and Sincerity

Since hajj is one of the greatest occasions for expressing one's humility before Allah Ta'ala, Rasulullah (sallallahu 'alaihi wasallam) rode on an old saddle. Furthermore, the padding which was placed on the saddle was so simple that it did not even equal four dirhams (silver coins).

Rasulullah (sallallahu 'alaihi wasallam) was concerned that his hajj must be solely for the pleasure of Allah Ta'ala and thus made du'aa in the following words,

« اَللّٰهُمَّ اجْعَلْهُ حَجًّا لَا رِيَاءَ فِيْهِ وَلَا سُمْعَةَ »

"O Allah! Make it a hajj in which there is no ostentation and no seeking of fame!" (Shamaa-il Tirmizi #335 and Sharhuz Zurqaani vol. 11, pg. 357)

If a person's intention is not pure (i.e. he is not performing hajj or 'umrah purely for the pleasure of Allah Ta'ala), then although he may be going to the holiest of places to fulfil a great 'ibaadah, his reward will be greatly decreased. In fact, he may even be taken to task by Allah Ta'ala. Hence, having the correct intention when performing hajj and 'umrah is essential.

Taking selfies throughout the auspicious journey of hajj and 'umrah and posting them on social network platforms, apart from being impermissible, goes totally against the spirit of sincerity which has been asked for in this prophetic du'aa. Engaging in this and in other sinful acts (such as missing salaah, intermingling of non-mahram men and women, etc.) are all factors that will cause one to be deprived of the great rewards and blessings of these blessed places.

Asmaa bintu 'Umais (radhiyallahu 'anha)

At the time of the Farewell Hajj, Sayyidah Asmaa bintu 'Umais (radhiyallahu 'anha) was married to Sayyiduna Abu Bakr (radhiyallahu 'anhu). While in Zul Hulaifah, Sayyidah Asmaa (radhiyallahu 'anha) was blessed with a son, Muhammad bin Abi Bakr (radhiyallahu 'anhuma).

After the child was born, on account of her being in the state of nifaas (post-natal bleeding), she sent a message to Rasulullah (sallallahu 'alaihi wasallam) asking, "What should I do?" Rasulullah (sallallahu 'alaihi wasallam) then instructed her to perform ghusl and enter into ihraam. *(Saheeh Muslim #2950)* However, she would not be allowed to make tawaaf until she becomes pure.

Talbiyah Aloud

Rasulullah (sallallahu 'alaihi wasallam) was reciting the talbiyah while he was traveling.

Jibreel ('alaihis salaam) also came to him and told him to instruct the Sahaabah (radhiyallahu 'anhum) to recite the talbiyah with raised voices. *(Sunan Nasaai #2753)*

Cupping at Malal

When Rasulullah (sallallahu 'alaihi wasallam) reached a place named Malal (which is approximately seventeen miles from Madeenah Munawwarah), he underwent cupping on the upper portion of his blessed foot.

لَبَّيْكَ اَللَّهُمَّ لَبَّيْكَ ، لَبَّيْكَ لَا شَرِيْكَ لَكَ لَبَّيْكَ ، إِنَّ الْحَمْدَ وَالنِّعْمَةَ لَكَ وَالْمُلْكَ ، لَا شَرِيْكَ لَكَ

Other Stops

Rowhaa - Second Stop

Rasulullah (sallallahu 'alaihi wasallam) next broke the journey and encamped at a place known as Rowhaa which is approximately seventy-four kilometres from Madeenah Munawwarah.

Regarding the valley of Rowhaa, Rasulullah (sallallahu 'alaihi wasallam) had mentioned, "It is one of the valleys of Jannah. Seventy Ambiyaa ('alaihimus salaam) had performed salaah in this masjid before me." *(Tabraani - Majma'uz Zawaaid #10005)*

While in Rowhaa, Rasulullah (sallallahu 'alaihi wasallam) saw a zebra that had been shot and killed by a hunter. The hunter then came before Rasulullah (sallallahu 'alaihi wasallam) and presented its meat to Rasulullah (sallallahu 'alaihi wasallam) and the Sahaabah (radhiyallahu 'anhum) as a gift. Rasulullah (sallallahu 'alaihi wasallam) accepted it, as the hunter was not in the state of ihraam. He then instructed Sayyiduna Abu Bakr (radhiyallahu 'anhu) to distribute the meat among the Sahaabah (radhiyallahu 'anhum). *(Sunan Nasaai #2818)*

Ithaabah – Third Stop

Rasulullah (sallallahu 'alaihi wasallam) thereafter continued until he reached a place named Ithaabah, where he found a buck that was lying in the shade of a sand dune, struck by an arrow but still alive.

Rasulullah (sallallahu 'alaihi wasallam) appointed a Sahaabi (radhiyallahu 'anhu) to stand guard over the buck until all the Sahaabah (radhiyallahu 'anhum) had passed by, to ensure that nobody ate from it (after it died), as it was not known as to whether the person who had hunted it had been in the state of ihraam or not, and also as the person who had shot it was now the owner of the buck. Hence, it was not permissible to eat from the buck without his permission. *(Sunan Nasaai #2818)*

'Arj – Fourth Stop

When Rasulullah (sallallahu 'alaihi wasallam) reached a place named Lahyay Jamal, he underwent cupping on his blessed head. *(Saheeh Bukhaari #1836)* He thereafter continued his journey and halted at a place named 'Arj.

The provisions of Rasulullah (sallallahu 'alaihi wasallam) and the provisions of Sayyiduna Abu Bakr (radhiyallahu 'anhu) were both on one camel which belonged to Sayyiduna Abu Bakr (radhiyallahu 'anhu).

Sayyiduna Abu Bakr (radhiyallahu 'anhu) was sitting, waiting for the slave to arrive with the provisions. However, when the slave arrived, Sayyiduna Abu Bakr (radhiyallahu 'anhu) saw that he did not have the camel with him. Sayyiduna Abu Bakr (radhiyallahu 'anhu) asked him where the camel was to which he replied, "I lost it last night."

Hearing this, Sayyiduna Abu Bakr (radhiyallahu 'anhu) became angry with the slave (as by losing the provisions of Rasulullah [sallallahu 'alaihi wasallam], he would cause inconvenience to him) and began to hit him saying, "It was just one camel and you lost it!" Rasulullah (sallallahu 'alaihi wasallam) smiled and remarked,

« اُنْظُرُوْا إِلٰى هٰذَا الْمُحْرِمِ مَا يَصْنَعُ »

"Look at this muhrim (person in ihraam) and how he is conducting."
(Sunan Abi Dawood #1818)

Although it was permissible for Sayyiduna Abu Bakr (radhiyallahu 'anhu) to discipline his slave, especially since it was not for any personal reason, rather because of the inconvenience which would be caused to Rasulullah (sallallahu 'alaihi wasallam) as a result of his negligence, Rasulullah (sallallahu 'alaihi wasallam) mentioned this statement in order to calm him down, as this type of behaviour was not in keeping with a person who is in the state of ihraam. Rasulullah (sallallahu 'alaihi wasallam) also said to him, "Take it easy, for the matter is not in your control, nor in our control."

When the family of Sayyiduna Fadhaalah Aslami (radhiyallahu 'anhu) heard that the provisions of Rasulullah (sallallahu 'alaihi wasallam) were lost, they immediately brought a container of hays (a dish made with dates, ghee and cheese)

and presented it to him. Rasulullah (sallallahu 'alaihi wasallam) called Sayyiduna Abu Bakr (radhiyallahu 'anhu) and said, "Come, O Abu Bakr (radhiyallahu 'anhu)! For Allah Ta'ala has sent us delicious breakfast!"

Sayyiduna Sa'd and Sayyiduna Abu Qays (radhiyallahu 'anhuma) also brought a camel bearing provisions and presented it to Rasulullah (sallallahu 'alaihi wasallam). However, Rasulullah (sallallahu 'alaihi wasallam) declined to accept it and made du'aa for Allah Ta'ala to bless them with barakah. (*Sharhuz Zurqaani vol. 11, pg. 359*)

Abwaa' – Fifth Stop

Rasulullah (sallallahu 'alaihi wasallam) thereafter halted at Abwaa'. It was in this place that the respected mother of Rasulullah (sallallahu 'alaihi wasallam) passed away and was buried.

According to some narrators, Rasulullah (sallallahu 'alaihi wasallam) halted in a place known as Waddaan. However, there is no contradiction, since Waddaan is actually a place in the valley of Abwaa'. Nowadays, Waddaan is known as Mastoorah and is approximately 228km from Madeenah Munawwarah.

'Usfaan – Sixth Stop

Rasulullah (sallallahu 'alaihi wasallam) next stopped at the valley of 'Usfaan which is approximately thirty-six miles from Makkah Mukarramah.

When he reached this valley, Rasulullah (sallallahu 'alaihi wasallam) asked Sayyiduna Abu Bakr (radhiyallahu 'anhu), "Which valley is this?" When Sayyiduna Abu Bakr (radhiyallahu 'anhu) replied that it was the valley of 'Usfaan, Rasulullah (sallallahu 'alaihi wasallam) said,

« لَقَدْ مَرَّ بِهِ هُودٌ وَصَالِحٌ عَلَى بَكَرَاتٍ حُمْرٍ خُطُمُهَا اللِّيْفُ ، أُزُرُهُمُ الْعَبَاءُ وَأَرْدِيَتُهُمُ النِّمَارُ ، يُلَبُّوْنَ يَحُجُّوْنَ الْبَيْتَ الْعَتِيْقَ »

"Nabi Hood and Nabi Saalih ('alaihimas salaam) passed it (i.e. this valley) riding on young, red camels which had reins of fiber. Their lower garments were of 'abaa (a certain type of clothing) and their upper garments were of a black and white striped material. They were reciting the talbiyah whilst proceeding to perform hajj of the old house (i.e. the Ka'bah)." (Musnad Ahmad #2067)

Sarif – Seventh Stop

Rasulullah (sallallahu 'alaihi wasallam) then came to Sarif, a place approximately six miles from Makkah Mukarramah.

It was in this very place that Rasulullah (sallallahu 'alaihi wasallam) had married Sayyidah Maimoonah (radhiyallahu 'anha) during 'Umratul Qadhaa, and it was here that he consummated the marriage with her thereafter, while returning to Madeenah Munawwarah from the 'Umratul Qadhaa. In the year 51 A.H., Sayyidah Maimoonah (radhiyallahu 'anha) passed away in this place and she was buried under the very tree beneath which her marriage was consummated.

While in Sarif, Rasulullah (sallallahu 'alaihi wasallam) said to the Sahaabah (radhiyallahu 'anhum),

« مَنْ لَمْ يَكُنْ مَعَهُ هَدْيٌ فَأَحَبَّ أَنْ يَجْعَلَهَا عُمْرَةً فَلْيَفْعَلْ ، وَمَنْ كَانَ مَعَهُ هَدْيٌ فَلَا »

"Whoever did not bring a hady (sacrificial) animal with him, and he wishes to make it an 'umrah (by changing his ihraam into the ihraam of just an 'umrah and cancelling the ihraam of hajj), then he may do so. However, the one who has brought a hady (sacrificial animal) with him may not do so." (Saheeh Bukhaari #1788)

The reason for Rasulullah (sallallahu 'alaihi wasallam) doing this was to abolish the belief that had existed since Jaahiliyyah (the pre-Islamic era), that 'umrah could not be performed during the months of hajj.

After Rasulullah (sallallahu 'alaihi wasallam) addressed the Sahaabah (radhiyallahu 'anhum), he went to Sayyidah 'Aaishah (radhiyallahu 'anha) and found her crying. When he asked her the reason for it, she explained that it was due to the fact that she would be unable to perform her 'umrah as a result of her not being in a state of offering salaah (since her menstrual period had commenced).

Rasulullah (sallallahu 'alaihi wasallam) comforted her by explaining that menstruation was something natural for women in general, and not something specific to her. Hence, she should not worry and stress about it. He further explained to her that her menstruation would not prevent her from carrying out the rituals of hajj, however, she would only be able to offer the tawaaf once she becomes pure. *(Saheeh Bukhaari #305 & #1788)*

Zu Tuwaa – Eight Stop

Rasulullah (sallallahu 'alaihi wasallam) then proceeded until he arrived in Zu Tuwaa. He spent the night preceding Sunday in this place. This was his last stop and it was from here that he departed for Makkah Mukarramah on Sunday after Fajr Salaah.

لَبَّيْكَ اَللّٰهُمَّ لَبَّيْكَ ، لَبَّيْكَ لَا شَرِيْكَ لَكَ لَبَّيْكَ ، إِنَّ الْحَمْدَ وَالنِّعْمَةَ لَكَ وَالْمُلْكَ ، لَا شَرِيْكَ لَكَ

Incidents Enroute

During the journey, the following two important incidents had also taken place, although their exact locations cannot be confirmed.

Anjashah (radhiyallahu 'anhu)

Sayyiduna Anjashah (radhiyallahu 'anhu) was a black slave of Rasulullah (sallallahu 'alaihi wasallam) who had a melodious voice. During this journey, he was leading the camels on which the blessed wives of Rasulullah (sallallahu 'alaihi wasallam) were seated. Once while leading them, he began chanting[3], thus making the camels increase their speed. Rasulullah (sallallahu 'alaihi wasallam) said to him,

《 وَيْحَكَ يَا أَنْجَشَةُ ، رُوَيْدَكَ سَوْقًا بِالْقَوَارِيرِ 》

"Woe to you O Anjashah! Be gentle when driving the glass bottles!"
(Saheeh Bukhaari #6149, Musnad Ahmad #26866 and Fat-hul Baari)

---

[3] The Arabs had a practice known as hudy, whereby they would chant to the camels, and this chanting would prompt and urge the camels to move faster.

In this hadeeth, Rasulullah (sallallahu 'alaihi wasallam) compared the women to glass bottles. There are two possible reasons for this:

a) Glass bottles are delicate and break easily. Hence, if the camels were carrying glass bottles, a fast pace would cause the bottles to break. Similarly, a fast pace can cause the women to be hurt, especially if they fall from the camel, as women are generally more 'delicate' (slight in built, etc.) compared to men and are thus more prone to injuries.

b) Glass is delicate and fragile and breaks easily without much effort. Similarly, a woman, by nature, is emotionally delicate (i.e. her emotions are more easily affected) and she is easily influenced by an attractive voice that has the potential to 'break' her taqwa just as glass is easily broken. *(Adapted from Fat-hul Baari)*

Rasulullah (sallallahu 'alaihi wasallam) was thus teaching the Ummah that utmost caution should be exercised in regard to purdah between men and women – even to the extent of purdah in voice – as they can easily be influenced and fall into sin.

When this was the caution that Rasulullah (sallallahu 'alaihi wasallam) exercised with a slave who was merely chanting to the camels in a sweet voice, how much more precaution should be exercised in today's times regarding women listening to the voices of men, when there is a fear that it would stir up their emotions?

Camel of Safiyyah (radhiyallahu 'anha)

While travelling, the camel of the respected wife of Rasulullah (sallallahu 'alaihi wasallam), Sayyidah Safiyyah (radhiyallahu 'anha), which was one of the best camels, kneeled due to sickness (and could not travel). She thus began to weep (in disappointment).

When Rasulullah (sallallahu 'alaihi wasallam) was informed of what had happened and learnt that she was weeping, he immediately came and began to comfort her and wipe her tears with his blessed hand. However, her weeping increased, and despite Rasulullah (sallallahu 'alaihi wasallam) telling her not to cry, she was unable to stop.

Rasulullah (sallallahu 'alaihi wasallam) thus instructed the Sahaabah (radhiyallahu 'anhum) to halt, although he initially had no intention of halting at that point. After halting, the tent of Rasulullah (sallallahu 'alaihi wasallam) was pitched. Rasulullah (sallallahu 'alaihi wasallam) then entered his tent.

That day was the turn of Sayyidah Safiyyah (radhiyallahu 'anha). Sayyidah Safiyyah (radhiyallahu 'anha) was worried, as she did not know whether her weeping had caused Rasulullah (sallallahu 'alaihi wasallam) to become upset with her.

She thus went to Sayyidah 'Aaishah (radhiyallahu 'anha) and said, "You know that I would never trade my day with Rasulullah (sallallahu 'alaihi wasallam) for anything in the world. However, I have given my day to you so that you can make Rasulullah (sallallahu 'alaihi wasallam) happy with me."

Sayyidah 'Aaishah (radhiyallahu 'anha) agreed and spent the day with Rasulullah (sallallahu 'alaihi wasallam,) thus bringing happiness to his blessed heart (as from all the respected wives, she was the most beloved wife to him).

When it was time to depart, Rasulullah (sallallahu 'alaihi wasallam) asked his respected wife, Sayyidah Zainab bintu Jahsh (radhiyallahu 'anha), to lend a spare camel of hers to Sayyidah Safiyyah (radhiyallahu 'anha). However, (out of possessiveness and the natural rivalry which exists between co-wives,) she said, "Should I give a camel to your Jewess[4]?"

Rasulullah (sallallahu 'alaihi wasallam) was extremely upset at this and thus ceased speaking to her and spending time with her for approximately two and a half months.

Nevertheless, (Sayyidah Zainab [radhiyallahu 'anha] repented for this statement that she uttered, and) shortly before his demise, Rasulullah (sallallahu 'alaihi wasallam) resumed coming to her and was pleased with her once more. *(Sunan Abi Dawood #4602 Musnad Ahmad #26866)*

This incident teaches us the importance of guarding the tongue and the seriousness of not being careful in our speech.

Another lesson learnt is that of becoming upset for the sake of Allah Ta'ala and Deen, and appropriately correcting the family members thereafter.

---

[4] The reason for her referring to Sayyidah Safiyyah (radhiyallahu 'anha) as a Jewess is that she was a Jewess before she accepted Islam and was honoured to enter the nikaah of Rasulullah (sallallahu 'alaihi wasallam).

Makkah Mukarramah

Ghusl

After performing the Fajr Salaah in Zu Tuwaa on Sunday 4th Zul Hijjah, Rasulullah (sallallahu 'alaihi wasallam) performed ghusl for entering Makkah Mukarramah.

Moosa ('alaihis salaam)

Rasulullah (sallallahu 'alaihi wasallam) thereafter proceeded, passing through the valley of Azraq. While passing through this valley, he (sallallahu 'alaihi wasallam) said,

« كَأَنِّيْ أَنْظُرُ إِلٰى مُوْسٰى عليه السلام هَابِطًا مِنَ الثَّنِيَّةِ ، وَلَهُ جُؤَارٌ إِلَى اللهِ بِالتَّلْبِيَةِ »

"It is as though I can see Nabi Moosa ('alaihis salaam), descending from the hill, calling out the talbiyah to Allah Ta'ala with a raised voice."[5]
(Saheeh Muslim #420)

---

[5] The commentators of hadeeth have given various explanations to this hadeeth. One of the preferred explanations is that perhaps Allah Ta'ala had shown Rasulullah (sallallahu 'alaihi wasallam) in his dream how Nabi Moosa ('alaihis salaam) had performed hajj in his era.

Entering

Rasulullah (sallallahu 'alaihi wasallam) entered Makkah Mukarramah during the day from the upper portion of Makkah Mukarramah. The area from which he (sallallahu 'alaihi wasallam) entered is currently known as Ma'aabid. This is where the king's palace is located and is also in the direction of Jannatul Mu'allaa.

When Rasulullah (sallallahu 'alaihi wasallam) entered Makkah Mukarramah, he first renewed his wudhu. *(Saheeh Bukhaari #1614 and Mirqaat vol. 5, pg. 459)*

He (sallallahu 'alaihi wasallam) thereafter entered the masjid at the time of dhuha (chaasht) from Baabus Salaam, which is also known as Baabu Bani Shaibah and Baabu 'Abdi Manaaf.

When Rasulullah (sallallahu 'alaihi wasallam) saw the Ka'bah, he faced it and engaged in du'aa.

Tawaaf

Rasulullah (sallallahu 'alaihi wasallam) thereafter performed his 'umrah.

When Rasulullah (sallallahu 'alaihi wasallam) came in-line with the Hajar Aswad, he made istilaam[6] by indicating towards it

---

[6] Istilaam means for one to stand facing the Hajr Aswad, place his hands on it, kiss it and recite, "Bimillahi Allahu Akbar". If this is diffuclt, one will touch it

using a stick and thereafter kissing the stick. This tawaaf was performed with idhtibaa'[7].

Rasulullah (sallallahu 'alaihi wasallam) performed this tawaaf and the subsequent sa'ee riding, not walking. The reasons for Rasulullah (sallallahu 'alaihi wasallam) performing this tawaaf and sa'ee while riding were multiple. They were:

a. Rasulullah (sallallahu 'alaihi wasallam) was not feeling well when he reached Makkah Mukarramah.

b. So that the people would be able to observe his actions and learn the method of tawaaf and sa'ee.

c. To make it easy for the people to address him and ask him their questions.

Whenever Rasulullah (sallallahu 'alaihi wasallam) would pass by the Hajar Aswad, he would make istilaam.

Two Rakaats and Zamzam

After performing tawaaf, Rasulullah (sallallahu 'alaihi wasallam) proceeded until he stood behind the Maqaam Ebrahim, with the Maqaam between him and the Ka'bah. Once at the Maqaam Ebrahim, he recited the following verse of the Quraan Majeed:

---

with an object, or face his hands towards it and thereafter kiss that object or his hands.

[7] Idhtibaa is for a man to tuck the ihraam sheet beneath his right arm and drape it over his left shoulder. In this manner, his right shoulder and right arm will be exposed.

$$\text{وَاتَّخِذُوا مِنْ مَّقَامِ اِبْرٰهِمَ مُصَلًّى}$$

And take from the Maqaam Ebrahim a place of salaah. (Surah Baqarah v125)

Rasulullah (sallallahu 'alaihi wasallam) then performed the two rakaats that are waajib after tawaaf. In the first rakaat, he (sallallahu 'alaihi wasallam) recited Surah Kaafiroon, and in the second rakaat, he (sallallahu 'alaihi wasallam) recited Surah Ikhlaas.

After performing the two rakaats, Rasulullah (sallallahu 'alaihi wasallam) made istilaam of the Hajar Aswad again and then proceeded to Mount Safaa through the door which was named Baabus Safaa.

Sa'ee

On nearing Mount Safaa, Rasulullah (sallallahu 'alaihi wasallam) recited the following verse:

$$\text{اِنَّ الصَّفَا وَالْمَرْوَةَ مِنْ شَعَآئِرِ اللهِ}$$

"Indeed, Safaa and Marwah are from the salient symbols of Allah." (Surah Baqarah v158)

Rasulullah (sallallahu 'alaihi wasallam) then said,

$$\text{«أَبْدَأُ بِمَا بَدَأَ اللهُ بِهِ»}$$

"I will commence (performing the sa'ee) with that which Allah Ta'ala commenced with (i.e. Allah Ta'ala mentioned Safaa first in the verse, so I will commence the sa'ee from Safaa)."

Rasulullah (sallallahu 'alaihi wasallam) then climbed Mount Safaa a little (until he could see the Ka'bah) and recited the following thrice:

» لَا إِلٰهَ إِلَّا اللهُ وَحْدَهُ لَا شَرِيْكَ لَهُ، لَهُ الْمُلْكُ وَلَهُ الْحَمْدُ وَهُوَ عَلٰى كُلِّ شَيْءٍ قَدِيْرٌ، لَا إِلٰهَ إِلَّا اللهُ وَحْدَهُ، أَنْجَزَ وَعْدَهُ وَنَصَرَ عَبْدَهُ وَهَزَمَ الْأَحْزَابَ وَحْدَهُ «

"There is none worthy of worship besides Allah Ta'ala, who is alone and has no partner. To Him alone belongs the kingdom, and to Him alone belongs all praise, and He has complete power over everything. There is none worthy of worship besides Allah Ta'ala, who is alone. He fulfilled His promise, and assisted His slave, and He alone defeated the groups (and armies of the disbelievers)."

Rasulullah (sallallahu 'alaihi wasallam) also engaged in du'aa.

He thereafter descended and began to walk towards Mount Marwah. On reaching Marwah, he carried out the same actions as he did at Safaa (i.e. he faced the Ka'bah, recited takbeer and engaged in du'aa).[8] *(Saheeh Muslim #2950)*

---

[8] The act of sa'ee and the running at the bottom of the valley is actually a remembrance of the sacrifice of Sayyidah Haajar ('alaihas salaam), when she ran desperately looking for water for her infant child, Nabi Ismaa'eel ('alaihis salaam). This action of hers, and her total submission to the command of Allah Ta'ala was so beloved and dear to Allah Ta'ala that He has made this an important ritual of hajj and 'umrah, despite thousands of years passing. This is a clear proof of the high position that Islam affords to women and the manner in which Islam appreciates their sacrifices and contributions.

Love and Obedience

In order to practically abolish the wrong belief of Jaahiliyyah regarding the impermissibility of 'umrah in the months of hajj, after completing his sa'ee, whilst Rasulullah (sallallahu 'alaihi wasallam) was still on Marwah, he commanded all those Sahaabah (radhiyallahu 'anhum) who did not bring a sacrificial animal with them to come out of their ihraam. None of the blessed wives of Rasulullah (sallallahu 'alaihi wasallam) had brought animals with and so they all exited their ihraam.

Thereafter, in order to emphasize to the Sahaabah (radhiyallahu 'anhum) that they were no longer in ihraam, Rasulullah (sallallahu 'alaihi wasallam) told them that they could even have relations with their wives.

Since Rasulullah (sallallahu 'alaihi wasallam) had brought along his sacrificial animals, he could not come out of ihraam. Such was the deep love of the Sahaabah (radhiyallahu 'anhum) for Rasulullah (sallallahu 'alaihi wasallam) that they wished to emulate him and resemble him in everything. Hence, they initially hesitated to come out of ihraam, as it would necessitate them being out of ihraam while Rasulullah (sallallahu 'alaihi wasallam) was still in ihraam. However, when Rasulullah (sallallahu 'alaihi wasallam) explained to them the reason for him remaining in ihraam, the Sahaabah (radhiyallahu 'anhum) wholeheartedly listened and obeyed.

Sayyiduna Suraaqah bin Maalik (radhiyallahu 'anhu) then asked Rasulullah (sallallahu 'alaihi wasallam) whether the law of performing 'umrah in the months of hajj was only allowed for that year, or whether it was allowed afterwards as well, until Qiyaamah. Rasulullah (sallallahu 'alaihi wasallam) replied that it was until Qiyaamah. *(Saheeh Muslim #2943 & #2950)*

Among the Sahaabah who did not come out of their ihraam (as they had brought along their sacrificial animals with them) were Sayyiduna Abu Bakr, Sayyiduna 'Umar, Sayyiduna 'Uthmaan, Sayyiduna 'Ali, Sayyiduna Zul Yasaarah, Sayyiduna Talhah and Sayyiduna Zubair (radhiyallahu 'anhum).

لَبَّيْكَ اللّٰهُمَّ لَبَّيْكَ ، لَبَّيْكَ لَا شَرِيْكَ لَكَ لَبَّيْكَ ، إِنَّ الْحَمْدَ وَالنِّعْمَةَ لَكَ وَالْمُلْكَ ، لَا شَرِيْكَ لَكَ

Abtah

Rasulullah (sallallahu 'alaihi wasallam) then settled on the outskirts of Makkah Mukarramah, in Abtah which is to the east of Makkah Mukarramah. He performed his salaah here for these four days as a musaafir.

During these days, Rasulullah (sallallahu 'alaihi wasallam) would come to the Haram to perform tawaaf.

Arrival of 'Ali (radhiyallahu 'anhu)

Sayyiduna 'Ali (radhiyallahu 'anhu) arrived from Yemen at this time and met Rasulullah (sallallahu 'alaihi wasallam) in Abtah. Rasulullah (sallallahu 'alaihi wasallam) had sent him to Yemen to collect zakaat from the Muslims of Yemen.

Sayyiduna 'Ali (radhiyallahu 'anhu) had brought with him thirty-seven of the hady (sacrificial) camels of Rasulullah (sallallahu 'alaihi wasallam), while Rasulullah (sallallahu 'alaihi wasallam) had brought sixty-three camels with him from Madeenah Munawwarah. Accordingly, the total number of the sacrificial animals of Rasulullah (sallallahu 'alaihi wasallam) was one hundred.

On his arrival, when Sayyiduna 'Ali (radhiyallahu 'anhu) saw his respected wife, Sayyidah Faatimah (radhiyallahu 'anha), he noticed that she was wearing dyed clothing and had applied surmah (antimony) to her eyes (i.e. she was carrying out actions which are regarded as violations of ihraam).

Since Sayyiduna 'Ali (radhiyallahu 'anhu) did not know that Rasulullah (sallallahu 'alaihi wasallam) had commanded the Sahaabah (radhiyallahu 'anhum) who did not have sacrificial animals to come out of ihraam (as he was still coming from Yemen at the time), he thought that she was committing a sin and reproached her. However, Sayyidah Faatimah (radhiyallahu 'anha) explained saying, "My father (sallallahu 'alaihi wasallam) commanded me to do this (come out of ihraam)."

Sayyiduna 'Ali (radhiyallahu 'anhu) then went to Rasulullah (sallallahu 'alaihi wasallam) to enquire whether Sayyidah Faatimah (radhiyallahu 'anha) was correct in what she had said. On hearing the incident, Rasulullah (sallallahu 'alaihi wasallam) said,

« صَدَقَتْ صَدَقَتْ »

"She has spoken the truth, she has spoken the truth." (Saheeh Muslim #2950)

Nevertheless, from this incident, we see the deep concern which the husband should have for the Deen of his wife. If the husband ever sees his wife carrying out any action or conducting herself in a manner that is displeasing to Allah Ta'ala, then he should immediately take the appropriate steps to correct her.

Visiting Sa'd (radhiyallahu 'anhu)

It was perhaps while Rasulullah (sallallahu 'alaihi wasallam) was in Abtah that he visited Sayyiduna Sa'd bin Abi Waqqaas (radhiyallahu 'anhu) who was so sick that he seemed to be on the verge of passing away.

During this visit, Sayyiduna Sa'd (radhiyallahu 'anhu) asked Rasulullah (sallallahu 'alaihi wasallam) whether he could make wasiyyah (a bequest) for all his wealth to be distributed in charity after his demise, since he was only leaving behind one daughter and she would not require the abundant wealth which he owned. However, Rasulullah (sallallahu 'alaihi wasallam) told him that his wasiyyah should not exceed one-third of his estate, and further said to him,

« إِنَّكَ أَنْ تَذَرَ وَرَثَتَكَ أَغْنِيَاءَ خَيْرٌ مِنْ أَنْ تَذَرَهُمْ عَالَةً يَتَكَفَّفُونَ النَّاسَ ، وَإِنَّكَ لَنْ تُنْفِقَ نَفَقَةً تَبْتَغِيْ بِهَا وَجْهَ اللهِ إِلَّا أُجِرْتَ حَتَّى مَا تَجْعَلُ فِيْ فِي امْرَأَتِكَ »

"Indeed, for you to leave your heirs wealthy (and self-sufficient) is better than you (giving all your wealth in charity and) leaving them in need, stretching their hands out to people. (Furthermore, if you are cured,) then whatever amount you spend to please Allah Ta'ala, you will be rewarded, even that (morsel) which you place in the mouth of your wife." (Saheeh Bukhaari #2742 & #6373)

Mina

Proceeding to Mina

On Thursday 8th Zul Hijjah, at the time of chaasht (mid-morning), Rasulullah (sallallahu 'alaihi wasallam) proceeded to Mina.

While going to Mina, Rasulullah (sallallahu 'alaihi wasallam) was accompanied by Sayyiduna Bilaal (radhiyallahu 'anhu) who was shading him with a cloth suspended on a stick.

Tying Ihraam

All those Sahaabah (radhiyallahu 'anhum) who had come out of ihraam after the 'umrah due to the command of Rasulullah (sallallahu 'alaihi wasallam) now tied their ihraam for hajj from Abtah, before going to Mina.

Five Salaahs

Rasulullah (sallallahu 'alaihi wasallam) performed Zuhr Salaah in Mina. He thereafter remained in Mina and spent the night in Mina as well. Hence, Rasulullah (sallallahu 'alaihi wasallam) performed five salaah in Mina in total at this time (i.e. from Zuhr on the 8th until Fajr on the 9th).

It was on this night that Surah Mursalaat was revealed.

لَبَّيْكَ اَللّٰهُمَّ لَبَّيْكَ ، لَبَّيْكَ لَا شَرِيْكَ لَكَ لَبَّيْكَ ، إِنَّ الْحَمْدَ وَالنِّعْمَةَ لَكَ وَالْمُلْكَ ، لَا شَرِيْكَ لَكَ

'Arafaat

Leaving Mina

The next morning, which was the morning of Friday, after the sun had risen, Rasulullah (sallallahu 'alaihi wasallam) set off for 'Arafaat. Rasulullah (sallallahu 'alaihi wasallam) travelled by the road known as 'Dhabb'.

Breaking the Custom of the Quraish

During the days of Jaahiliyyah, the Quraish would encamp at a place called Mash'arul Haraam in Muzdalifah (which is between Mina and 'Arafaat), while the rest of the people would proceed further and encamp at 'Arafaat.

The reason that the Quraish would present for remaining in Muzadalifah was that they were the custodians and guardians of the Ka'bah Shareef. Hence, it was inappropriate for them to leave the boundaries of the Haram (Muzdalifah is within the boundary while 'Arafaat is out of the Haram).

The Quraish were convinced that Rasulullah (sallallahu 'alaihi wasallam) would encamp in Muzdalifah, as they would do.

However Allah Ta'ala revealed the verse of the Quraan Majeed that commanded Rasulullah (sallallahu 'alaihi wasallam) to proceed beyond Muzdalifah until he reached 'Arafaat. *(Saheeh Bukhaari #4520)* The verse was:

$$ثُمَّ اَفِيْضُوْا مِنْ حَيْثُ اَفَاضَ النَّاسُ$$

"Then depart (for Muzdalifah) from the place from where all the people depart (i.e. 'Arafaat)." (Surah Baqarah v199)

When Allah Ta'ala instructed Rasulullah (sallallahu 'alaihi wasallam) to leave from 'Arafaat, he will have to obviously first go there in order to be able to leave from there.

In fulfilling this command of Allah Ta'ala, whilst still in Mina, Rasulullah (sallallahu 'alaihi wasallam) instructed that a tent be pitched for him at Namirah (on the border of 'Arafaat, where the masjid of 'Arafaat currently stands). Thus, when Rasulullah (sallallahu 'alaihi wasallam) came to Namirah, he found that a tent had been pitched for him according to his instruction. *(Saheeh Muslim #2950)*

Historic Khutbah

After zawaal (midday), Rasulullah (sallallahu 'alaihi wasallam) commanded that his camel, Qaswaa should be saddled for him. Then he left Namirah and came to the bottom of the valley, which is known as 'Urnah, where he delivered a historic khutbah to the Sahaabah (radhiyallahu 'anhum).

As mentioned earlier, Rasulullah (sallallahu 'alaihi wasallam) left this world eighty-one days after this day of 'Arafah. Furthermore, it was an occasion at which more than one hundred thousand Sahaabah (radhiyallahu 'anhum) were present. Thus, the advices which Rasulullah (sallallahu 'alaihi wasallam) gave on this momentous occasion were extremely comprehensive, pertinent and are regarded as parting advices.

Rasulullah (sallallahu 'alaihi wasallam) addressed the Sahaabah (radhiyallahu 'anhum) saying,

Sanctity of a Muslim

« إِنَّ دِمَاءَكُمْ وَأَمْوَالَكُمْ حَرَامٌ عَلَيْكُمْ كَحُرْمَةِ يَوْمِكُمْ هٰذَا فِىْ شَهْرِكُمْ هٰذَا فِىْ بَلَدِكُمْ هٰذَا »

"Indeed, your blood and wealth are sacred (i.e. haraam for another person to violate) upon you, just like the sanctity of this day of yours, in this month of yours, in this place of yours."

The honour of the occasion was compounded by it deriving honour through multiple aspects, i.e. it was a day in which fighting was not allowed, it was a place (the Haram) in which fighting was not allowed and it was also a month in which fighting was not allowed. Despite the occasion enjoying sanctity from three separate dimensions, the sanctity of a Muslim was still shown to be greater.

Aspects of Ignorance

« أَلَا كُلُّ شَىْءٍ مِنْ أَمْرِ الْجَاهِلِيَّةِ تَحْتَ قَدَمَىَّ مَوْضُوْعٌ »

"Behold! Everything pertaining to the (wrong) aspects of the days of ignorance is abolished under my feet."

» وَدِمَاءُ الْجَاهِلِيَّةِ مَوْضُوْعَةٌ ، وَإِنَّ أَوَّلَ دَمٍ أَضَعُ مِنْ دِمَائِنَا دَمُ ابْنِ رَبِيْعَةَ بْنِ الْحَارِثِ «

"The blood of the days of ignorance is cancelled, and the first blood that I cancel from our blood (i.e. the blood of our family) is the blood of the son of Rabee'ah bin Haarith."

Cancelling the blood of the time of Jaahiliyyah means that if someone killed another pre-Islam, neither will he be killed in retaliation, nor will blood money be taken from him now.

Sayyiduna Rabee'ah (radhiyallahu 'anhu) was the son of Haarith bin 'Abdil Muttalib, the paternal uncle of Rasulullah (sallallahu 'alaihi wasallam). Sayyiduna Rabee'ah (radhiyallahu 'anhu) was thus the first cousin of Rasulullah (sallallahu 'alaihi wasallam). He had an infant child named Iyaas, whom he had left with the Banu Sa'd tribe to be suckled and raised in the countryside (as was done with Rasulullah [sallallahu 'alaihi wasallam] himself when he was an infant).

However, a battle broke out between the Banu Sa'd and Huzail tribes, and during the battle, a person from Huzail threw a stone which struck the infant Iyaas as he was crawling between the homes. This stone caused his death, due to which the Huzail owed blood money. In this khutbah, Rasulullah (sallallahu 'alaihi wasallam) cancelled all blood monies outstanding from Jaahiliyyah – commencing with this blood money which was due to his own family. (*Mirqaat vol. 5, pg. 437*)

« وَرِبَا الْجَاهِلِيَّةِ مَوْضُوْعٌ ، وَأَوَّلُ رِبًا أَضَعُ رِبَانَا رِبَا عَبَّاسِ بْنِ عَبْدِ الْمُطَّلِبِ ، فَإِنَّهُ مَوْضُوْعٌ كُلُّهُ »

"The interest of the days of ignorance is cancelled[9], and the first interest that I cancel is our interest (i.e. the interest of our family member), the interest of 'Abbaas bin 'Abdil Muttalib (radhiyallahu 'anhu), for his interest has been cancelled entirely (i.e. the interest and the loan amount have both been cancelled)."

On this occasion, Rasulullah (sallallahu 'alaihi wasallam) ruled that all the interest monies that were being owed to people from loans issued during the pre-Islamic era will fall off, i.e. only the initial loan amount will be repaid and no interest will be paid. However, when it came to his uncle, Sayyiduna 'Abbaas bin 'Abdil Muttalib (radhiyallahu 'anhu), then Rasulullah (sallallahu 'alaihi wasallam) cancelled even the initial loan amount so that nothing would be owed to him. *(Ad-Durrul Mandood vol. 3, pg. 255)*

The fact that Rasulullah (sallallahu 'alaihi wasallam) first cancelled the blood money and interest which were due to his own family, explains the important principle that when a person is advising others, he should first ensure that he and his family are conforming to that advice, since this will have a greater effect on others. *(Sharhun Nawawi - Saheeh Muslim vol. 1, pg. 397)*

---

[9] For a person of imaan, merely the fact that his Allah and Rasul (sallallahu 'alaihi wasallam) have prohibited something should be sufficient as a deterrent. However, the aspect of interest is so severe that Allah Ta'ala has announced war with such a person. Further, all those who are associated with the transaction have been cursed by Rasulullah (sallallahu 'alaihi wasallam). How can one ever be successful and prosperous when he is at war with Allah Ta'ala and earning the curse of Rasulullah (sallallahu 'alaihi wasallam)?

Treatment of Wives

« فَاتَّقُوا اللهَ فِي النِّسَاءِ ، فَإِنَّكُمْ أَخَذْتُمُوهُنَّ بِأَمَانِ اللهِ ، وَاسْتَحْلَلْتُمْ فُرُوجَهُنَّ بِكَلِمَةِ اللهِ »

"Fear Allah Ta'ala regarding women, for you have taken them (into your nikaah) with the trust of Allah Ta'ala (i.e. they are an amaanah from Allah Ta'ala) and you have made relations with them halaal through the words of Allah Ta'ala (as the name of Allah Ta'ala is taken at the time of nikaah)."

Unfortunately, some men take advantage of the submissive and weak nature of women. By saying "fear Allah Ta'ala regarding women", Rasulullah (sallallahu 'alaihi wasallam) is impressing upon men that although you may have some authority over them, Allah Ta'ala has complete authority over you, hence you should fear Him in the manner in which you treat them.

Another narration states: "Fear Allah Ta'ala regarding women for they are like captives with you (i.e. bound to you through nikaah). They do not possess anything of their own (i.e. they are generally dependent on their husbands to support them), and they have rights over you and you have rights over them." (Musnad Ahmad #20695)

He further explained that "you have taken them with the trust of Allah Ta'ala". Hence, just as an amaanah (trust) cannot be abused, these women are an amaanah from Allah Ta'ala and cannot be abused.

Furthermore, just as a Muslim will not speak a lie after taking the name of Allah Ta'ala, as he respects the sanctity of Allah Ta'ala's name, he should respect his nikaah and not use it to abuse his wife, as his nikaah was performed with the name of Allah Ta'ala as well.

An important point to take note of is that Islam has given such status to women, that even during this momentous occasion, Rasulullah (sallallahu 'alaihi wasallam) instructed the men to fear Allah Ta'ala regarding the manner in which they treat their wives.

Right of Husbands

« وَلَكُمْ عَلَيْهِنَّ أَنْ لَا يُوَطِّئْنَ فُرُشَكُمْ أَحَدًا تَكْرَهُوْنَهُ »

"It is your right over them that they do not allow anyone that you do not approve of to trample your bedding (i.e. to enter your home)."

In the pre-Islamic era, even when the husband would be away from home, his wife would allow other men into the home to sit and speak with her. In this way, a strange man (not her mahram) would sit with her in privacy and conduct a casual conversation.

In this khutbah, Rasulullah (sallallahu 'alaihi wasallam) condemned this practice of Jaahiliyyah and explained that the laws of hijaab and niqaab must be upheld. Hence, there must be total segregation between non-mahram men and women.

This could also apply to chatting with non-mahram males via social networks, which has become extremely common nowadays.

In another narration, Raslulullah (sallallahu 'alaihi wasallam) mentioned another right of the husband over his wife in the following words: "And they will not disobey you in permissible matters." *(Bazzaar - Majma'uz Zawaaid #5688)* Rasulullah (sallallahu 'alaihi wasallam) thus highlighted that a wife must obey her husband. However, he (sallallahu 'alaihi wasallam) clearly explained that she will only obey him in permissible matters. Hence, the husband cannot force her to comply with him in impermissible things, e.g. forcing her to dress attractively out of the home, attend mixed gatherings, and carry out haraam actions in the bedroom, etc.

Rights of Wives

« وَلَهُنَّ عَلَيْكُمْ رِزْقُهُنَّ وَكِسْوَتُهُنَّ بِالْمَعْرُوفِ »

"And it is their right over you that you provide them with their food and clothing in a good manner."

Rasulullah (sallallahu 'alaihi wasallam) made it clear that it is the responsibility of the husband to provide for the wife. Hence, it is incorrect for the husband to make his wife toil and slog in his business, or encourage or force her to seek employment to supplement the income.

When this is done, the poor woman is abused as she has to work, see to her domestic responsibilities and also see to the upbringing of her children. She is thus burdened with both her responsibility and her husband's responsibility. Another serious problem is the violation of the laws of sharee'ah (e.g. laws of hijaab and niqaab) that are commonly violated in the workplace.

Book of Allah

« وَقَدْ تَرَكْتُ فِيكُمْ مَا لَنْ تَضِلُّوا بَعْدَهُ إِنِ اعْتَصَمْتُمْ بِهِ ، كِتَابُ اللهِ »

"I have left with you that which if you hold fast to it, you would never go astray after (holding to) it - the Book of Allah."

Apart from adhering to the shar'ee laws and injunctions which are contained in the Quraan Majeed (such as the laws of salaah, fasting, zakaat, hajj, talaaq, etc.), holding on firmly to the Quraan Majeed will also include following the commands of the Quraan Majeed in regard to one's character (showing kindness to relatives, neighbours, etc.), refraining from sins and reforming one's life, etc.

In essence, holding on firmly to the Quraan Majeed entails holding on firmly to the entire Deen. So long as one holds on firmly to Deen, one will remain rightly guided and will be on the path to Jannah.

Conveyed the Message

Rasulullah (sallallahu 'alaihi wasallam) thereafter asked the Sahaabah (radhiyallahu 'anhum),

« وَأَنْتُمْ تُسْأَلُونَ عَنِّي ، فَمَا أَنْتُمْ قَائِلُونَ ؟ »

"You would be asked about me (on the Day of Judgement), so what would you say?"

The Sahaabah (radhiyallahu 'anhum) said: "We will bear witness that you have conveyed (the message), fulfilled (your responsibility) and wished well."

On hearing this reply from his Sahaabah (radhiyallahu 'anhum), Rasulullah (sallallahu 'alaihi wasallam) raised his forefinger towards the sky and pointed it at the people and said thrice,

« اَللّٰهُمَّ اشْهَدْ ، اَللّٰهُمَّ اشْهَدْ »

"O Allah, you bear witness. O Allah, you bear witness (that they have testified that I have conveyed the message)." (Saheeh Muslim #2950)

Not Fasting

Some Sahaabah (radhiyallahu 'anhum) were unsure whether Rasulullah (sallallahu 'alaihi wasallam) was fasting on the day of 'Arafah.

In order to clarify the matter, Sayyidah Ummul Fadhl (radhiyallahu 'anha), the wife of Sayyiduna 'Abbaas (radhiyallahu 'anhu), sent a bowl of milk to Rasulullah (sallallahu 'alaihi wasallam). When Rasulullah (sallallahu 'alaihi wasallam) received the milk, he drank it. Since he was seated on his she-camel, all of them could clearly see him, and they thus came to know that he was not fasting. *(Saheeh Bukhaari #1661)*

Joining Zuhr and 'Asr

After the khutbah was delivered, Rasulullah (sallallahu 'alaihi wasallam) instructed Sayyiduna Bilaal (radhiyallahu 'anhu) to call out the azaan.

Rasulullah (sallallahu 'alaihi wasallam) then performed the Zuhr Salaah, and immediately thereafter, performed the 'Asr Salaah with that one azaan in the time of Zuhr. However, there was a separate iqaamah called out for the two salaahs.

NB: According to the Hanafi Mazhab, there are certain conditions for the permissibility of joining Zuhr and 'Asr Salaah in 'Arafaat.

Wuqoof and Du'aa

Rasulullah (sallallahu 'alaihi wasallam) then rode his she-camel, Qaswaa and proceeded to Jabalur Rahmah, the mountain which is situated in the middle of 'Arafaat. *(Fat hul Mulhim vol. 3, pg. 286)*

Here he made his she-camel, Qaswaa stand in such a position that its stomach was in line with the rocks at the foot of the mountain and the pathway which was used by those who go on foot was in front of him, whilst he was facing towards the qiblah. He then began to engage in du'aa; beseeching and imploring Allah Ta'ala. *(Saheeh Muslim #2950)*

The following narrations mention some of the du'aas which Rasulullah (sallallahu 'alaihi wasallam) made on this blessed and auspicious occasion:

1. Rasulullah (sallallahu 'alaihi wasallam) said, "The best du'aa is the du'aa (which is made) on the Day of 'Arafah, and the best (words) which I and the Ambiyaa ('alaihimus salaam) before me have said (on the Day of 'Arafah) is (the following words),

« لَا إِلَهَ إِلَّا اللهُ وَحْدَهُ لَا شَرِيْكَ لَهُ لَهُ الْمُلْكُ وَلَهُ الْحَمْدُ وَهُوَ عَلَى كُلِّ شَيْءٍ قَدِيْرٌ »

'There is none worthy of worship besides Allah Ta'ala, Who is alone and has no partner. To Him alone belongs the kingdom, and to Him alone belongs all praise, and He has complete power over everything.'"

(Sunan Tirmizi #3585)

2. Sayyiduna 'Ali (radhiyallahu 'anhu) said, "The du'aa which Rasulullah (sallallahu 'alaihi wasallam) made the most on the late-afternoon of 'Arafah in the place of wuqoof was,

« اَللّٰهُمَّ لَكَ الْحَمْدُ كَالَّذِيْ تَقُوْلُ وَخَيْرًا مِّمَّا نَقُوْلُ ، اَللّٰهُمَّ لَكَ صَلَاتِيْ وَنُسُكِيْ وَمَحْيَايَ وَمَمَاتِيْ وَإِلَيْكَ مَآبِيْ وَلَكَ رَبِّ تُرَاثِيْ ، اَللّٰهُمَّ إِنِّيْ أَعُوْذُ بِكَ مِنْ عَذَابِ الْقَبْرِ وَوَسْوَسَةِ الصَّدْرِ وَشَتَاتِ الْأَمْرِ ، اَللّٰهُمَّ إِنِّيْ أَسْئَلُكَ مِنْ خَيْرِ مَا تَجِيْئُ بِهِ الرِّيَاحُ وَأَعُوْذُ بِكَ مِنْ شَرِّ مَا تَجِيْئُ بِهِ الرِّيَاحُ »

'O Allah! Praises are for You as You have expressed and much more than what we can ever express. O Allah! For You is my salaah, my sacrifice (or worship), my life and my death and to You is my ultimate return and all my assets (eventually) belong to You. O Allah! I seek Your protection from the punishment of the grave, the whispers of the heart and from disarray (and complication) in my affairs. O Allah! I beg of You all the good which is brought by the winds and I seek Your protection from all the evil which the winds carry.'"

(Sunan Tirmizi #3520 and Shu'abul Imaan #3560)

3. Sayyiduna 'Abdullah bin 'Abbaas (radhiyallahu 'anhuma) said, "Amongst the du'aas which Rasulullah (sallallahu 'alaihi wasallam) made in his hajj on the late-afternoon of 'Arafah was,

« اَللّٰهُمَّ إِنَّكَ تَسْمَعُ كَلَامِيْ وَتَرَى مَكَانِيْ وَتَعْلَمُ سِرِّيْ وَعَلَانِيَتِيْ ، لَا يَخْفٰى عَلَيْكَ شَيْءٌ مِنْ أَمْرِيْ ، وَأَنَا الْبَائِسُ الْفَقِيْرُ الْمُسْتَغِيْثُ الْمُسْتَجِيْرُ الْوَجِلُ الْمُشْفِقُ الْمُقِرُّ الْمُعْتَرِفُ بِذَنْبِهٖ ، أَسْأَلُكَ مَسْأَلَةَ الْمِسْكِيْنِ ، وَأَبْتَهِلُ إِلَيْكَ ابْتِهَالَ الْمُذْنِبِ الذَّلِيْلِ ، وَأَدْعُوْكَ دُعَاءَ الْخَائِفِ الضَّرِيْرِ ، مَنْ خَضَعَتْ لَكَ رَقَبَتُهُ وَفَاضَتْ لَكَ عَبْرَتُهُ وَذَلَّ لَكَ جِسْمُهُ وَرَغِمَ لَكَ أَنْفُهُ ، اَللّٰهُمَّ لَا تَجْعَلْنِيْ بِدُعَائِكَ شَقِيًّا وَكُنْ بِيْ رَؤُوْفًا رَحِيْمًا ، يَا خَيْرَ الْمَسْئُوْلِيْنَ وَ يَا خَيْرَ الْمُعْطِيْنَ »

'O Allah! Indeed, You hear my speech and You see my place (where I am), You know what I conceal and what I reveal. None of my affairs are hidden from You. I am the desperate one, the needy one, the one who is crying out for help, the one who is seeking refuge, the fearful one, the one who is in awe (of You), the one who confesses and admits his sins. I beg of You the begging of the destitute, and I implore You the imploring of the disgraceful sinner. I call onto You the calling of the fearful afflicted person, the one whose neck is lowered (in submission) before You, whose eyes pour out tears before You, whose body is humbled and whose nose is soiled in dust before You. O Allah! Do not make me a deprived one in my du'aa to You. Be kind and merciful to me. O the best of those who are asked and O the best of those who grant.'"
(Tabraani - Majma'uz Zawaaid #5613 and Al-Ahaadeethul Mukhtaarah li Dhiyaa Al-Maqdisi #233)

4. Rasulullah (sallallahu 'alaihi wasallam) begged Allah Ta'ala for the forgiveness of his Ummah. Allah Ta'ala informed Rasulullah (sallallahu 'alaihi wasallam),

« إِنِّيْ قَدْ غَفَرْتُ لَهُمْ مَا خَلَا الظَّالِمَ ، فَإِنِّيْ آخُذُ لِلْمَظْلُوْمِ مِنْهُ »

"I have forgiven them, except for the oppressor, as I will hold him accountable for the sake of the one who was oppressed."

Such was the concern of Rasulullah (sallallahu 'alaihi wasallam) for even the oppressor of his Ummah, that he responded,

« أَيْ رَبِّ إِنْ شِئْتَ أَعْطَيْتَ الْمَظْلُوْمَ مِنَ الْجَنَّةِ وَغَفَرْتَ لِلظَّالِمِ »

"O my Rabb! If you wish, you can give the oppressed one (bounties and ranks) from Jannah (to compensate him for undergoing oppression) and forgive the oppressor!"

This du'aa of Rasulullah (sallallahu 'alaihi wasallam) for the oppressor of the Ummah was not accepted at this time. However, it was accepted the next morning in Muzdalifah. (Sunan Ibni Maajah #3013)

Perfection of Deen

The following verse of the Quraan Majeed was revealed after 'Asr Salaah while Rasulullah (sallallahu 'alaihi wasallam) was seated on his camel. On account of the weight of the wahi, the camel was forced to kneel.

اَلْيَوْمَ اَكْمَلْتُ لَكُمْ دِيْنَكُمْ وَاَتْمَمْتُ عَلَيْكُمْ نِعْمَتِيْ وَرَضِيْتُ لَكُمُ الْاِسْلَامَ دِيْنًا

"Today I have perfected your Deen for you, completed My favour upon you, and I am pleased with Islam as your religion." (Surah Maa-idah v3)

When this verse was revealed, Sayyiduna 'Umar (radhiyallahu 'anhu) began to weep. When Rasulullah (sallallahu 'alaihi wasallam) asked him why he was weeping, he replied, "The thing which is making me weep is that we were increasing in our Deen. However, when Deen is complete, then all things begin to decrease after reaching completion." Hearing his reply,

Rasulullah (sallallahu 'alaihi wasallam) confirmed that what he had said was indeed true. *(Musannaf Ibni Abi Shaibah #35549)*

It was as though Sayyiduna 'Umar (radhiyallahu 'anhu) had perceived, through this verse of the Quraan Majeed, that when the Deen of Islam was now perfect and complete, then the time for Rasulullah's (sallallahu 'alaihi wasallam) departure had drawn near, as he had completed his mission.

Ka'b Ahbaar (rahimahullah), who was previously a leading Jewish scholar, once came to Sayyiduna 'Umar (radhiyallahu 'anhu) (before accepting Islam) and said, "O Ameerul Mumineen! There is a verse in your Quraan Majeed which you recite, if it was revealed to us, the Jews, we would have made the day of its revelation an 'Eid (celebration)."

When Sayyiduna 'Umar (radhiyallahu 'anhu) asked him as to which verse he was referring to, he replied by quoting the abovementioned verse.

Sayyiduna 'Umar (radhiyallahu 'anhu) then said, "We know the day and place in which it was revealed to Rasulullah (sallallahu 'alaihi wasallam). (It was revealed to him) whilst he was standing in 'Arafah on the Day of Jumu'ah." *(Saheeh Bukhaari #45 and Fat-hul Baari)*

In another narration, Sayyiduna 'Umar (radhiyallahu 'anhu) said, "It descended on an occasion that was a double 'Eid; the Day of Jumu'ah and the Day of 'Arafah." *(Sunan Tirmizi #3044)*

Boasting about the Sahaabah (radhiyallahu 'anhum)

It was on this evening of 'Arafah, that Allah Ta'ala boasted to His angels about the Sahaabah (radhiyallahu 'anhum) in general and about Sayyiduna 'Umar (radhiyallahu 'anhu) in particular.

Sayyiduna 'Abdullah bin 'Abbaas (radhiyallahu 'anhuma) narrates that once Rasulullah (sallallahu 'alaihi wasallam) looked at Sayyiduna 'Umar (radhiyallahu 'anhu) and smiled at him. He (sallallahu 'alaihi wasallam) then asked,

« يَا ابْنَ الْخَطَّابِ ! مِمَّ تَبَسَّمْتُ إِلَيْكَ ؟ »

"O son of Khattaab, do you know why I smiled at you?"

Sayyiduna 'Umar (radhiyallahu 'anhu) replied, "Allah Ta'ala and His Rasul (sallallahu 'alaihi wasallam) know best." Rasulullah (sallallahu 'alaihi wasallam) then explained,

« إِنَّ اللهَ عَزَّ وَجَلَّ بَاهَى بِأَهْلِ عَرَفَةَ عَامَّةً ، وَبَاهَى بِكَ خَاصَّةً »

"Allah Ta'ala boasted (to His angels on the evening of 'Arafah) about the people (who had converged) at 'Arafah in general, and boasted about you in particular." (Tabraani - Majma'uz Zawaaid #14448)

Allah Ta'ala boasting to His angels about all the Sahaabah (radhiyallahu 'anhum) in general and about Sayyiduna 'Umar (radhiyallahu 'anhu) in particular was a divine sanction that He would remain pleased with them throughout their lives.

Muzdalifah

Departure from 'Arafaat

After sunset, Rasulullah (sallallahu 'alaihi wasallam) departed from 'Arafaat to Muzdalifah without performing the Maghrib Salaah.

Rasulullah (sallallahu 'alaihi wasallam) placed Sayyiduna Usaamah bin Zaid (radhiyallahu 'anhuma) on the camel behind him and travelled on the road known as 'Ma-zimayn'.

Traveling with Calmness

Rasulullah (sallallahu 'alaihi wasallam) held the reins of his she-camel so tightly that her head touched the saddle, in order to keep her under control, so that she moves calmly and does not run. However, whenever she reached an incline, he loosened the reins slightly to make it easier for her to ascend. *(Saheeh Muslim #2950)*

Whilst departing from 'Arafaat, Rasulullah (sallallahu 'alaihi wasallam) heard behind him the sounds of people shouting and hitting their camels, so he indicated towards them with his whip and said,

«أَيُّهَا النَّاسُ عَلَيْكُمْ بِالسَّكِينَةِ ، فَإِنَّ الْبِرَّ لَيْسَ بِالْإِيْضَاعِ»

"O people! Observe (travelling with) calmness, for indeed piety is not in hastening (i.e. there is no reward in doing so)." (Saheeh Bukhaari #1671)

Dismounting

While on the road, Rasulullah (sallallahu 'alaihi wasallam) dismounted on the left of the road at the valley of Azaakhir and relieved himself by passing water. He (sallallahu 'alaihi wasallam) then made a quick wudhu.

Sayyiduna Usaamah (radhiyallahu 'anhu) asked Rasulullah (sallallahu 'alaihi wasallam) regarding performing Maghrib Salaah. Rasulullah (sallallahu 'alaihi wasallam) replied that they would perform it ahead.

Rasulullah (sallallahu 'alaihi wasallam) then reached Muzdalifah. *(Saheeh Bukhaari #1671 and Sharhuz Zurqaani vol. 11, pg. 413)*

Joining Salaahs and Sleeping

Upon reaching Muzdalifah, Rasulullah (sallallahu 'alaihi wasallam) performed Maghrib Salaah and 'Esha Salaah in the time of 'Esha.

Rasulullah (sallallahu 'alaihi wasallam) thereafter slept and did not spend this night in 'ibaadah. This was perhaps on account of the exertion in du'aa in 'Arafaat and the travelling to Muzdalifah, and also considering the actions that would be carried out the following day i.e. pelting, slaughtering, tawaaf, etc. *(Sharhuz Zurqaani vol. 11, pg. 415)*

Women and Children

Rasulullah (sallallahu 'alaihi wasallam) permitted those who were weak from his family (e.g. some women and children) to proceed early to Mina.

Among these were Sayyidah Saudah (radhiyallahu 'anha), Sayyidah Ummu Salamah (radhiyallahu 'anha) and Sayyidah Ummu Habeebah (radhiyallahu 'anha). Rasulullah (sallallahu 'alaihi wasallam) sent Sayyiduna 'Abbaas (radhiyallahu 'anhu) and his son, Sayyiduna 'Abdullah (radhiyallahu 'anhu) to accompany the women and children to Mina. They were instructed not to pelt before sunrise.

Pebbles and Wuqoof

Rasulullah (sallallahu 'alaihi wasallam) performed Fajr Salaah at the earliest time and then mounted his she-camel, Qaswaa. He instructed his cousin, Sayyiduna Fadhl bin 'Abbaas (radhiyallahu 'anhuma), to collect pebbles for him (to pelt the jamaraat).

He (sallallahu 'alaihi wasallam) thereafter proceeded to the mountain in Muzdalifah, known as Mash'arul Haraam. Here, Rasulullah (sallallahu 'alaihi wasallam) faced the qiblah and performed wuqoof, engaging in du'aa, praising Allah Ta'ala and zikr, until it became bright. *(Saheeh Muslim #2950 and Sharhuz Zurqaani vol. 11, pg. 425)*

Acceptance of Du'aa

Rasulullah (sallallahu 'alaihi wasallam) repeated the du'aa for the forgiveness of his Ummah. This du'aa of Rasulullah (sallallahu 'alaihi wasallam) was now accepted for even the oppressor, due to which Rasulullah (sallallahu 'alaihi wasallam) smiled. Noticing this, Sayyiduna Abu Bakr and Sayyiduna 'Umar (radhiyallahu 'anhuma) asked Rasulullah (sallallahu 'alaihi wasallam), "May my mother and father be sacrificed for you! This is not a time during which you would normally smile, so what is it that caused you to smile? – May Allah Ta'ala always keep you (happy and) smiling."

Rasulullah (sallallahu 'alaihi wasallam) explained,

« إِنَّ عَدُوَّ اللهِ إِبْلِيْسَ لَمَّا عَلِمَ أَنَّ اللهَ عَزَّ وَجَلَّ قَدِ اسْتَجَابَ دُعَائِيْ وَغَفَرَ لِأُمَّتِيْ أَخَذَ التُّرَابَ فَجَعَلَ يَحْثُوْهُ عَلَى رَأْسِهِ وَيَدْعُوْ بِالْوَيْلِ وَالثُّبُوْرِ ، فَأَضْحَكَنِيْ مَا رَأَيْتُ مِنْ جَزَعِهِ »

"When the enemy of Allah, Iblees, came to know that Allah 'Azza wa Jall answered my du'aa and forgave my Ummah, he took sand and began to throw it over his head, asking to be destroyed and perished (as his efforts were now wasted). It was the sight of his anguish that caused me to smile." (Sunan Ibni Maajah #3013)

This forgiveness refers to those oppressors who sincerely repent and are genuinely unable to fulfil the right that they owe to others. They also have the firm resolve that in the event of them being able to fulfil it in the future, they will definitely do so. *(Sharhuz Zurqaani vol. 11, pg. 418)*

لَبَّيْكَ اَللّٰهُمَّ لَبَّيْكَ ، لَبَّيْكَ لَا شَرِيْكَ لَكَ لَبَّيْكَ ، إِنَّ الْحَمْدَ وَالنِّعْمَةَ لَكَ وَالْمُلْكَ ، لَا شَرِيْكَ لَكَ

10ᵗʰ Zul Hijjah

Departure from Muzdalifah

Rasulullah (sallallahu 'alaihi wasallam) then departed from Muzdalifah before sunrise, with Sayyiduna Fadhl bin 'Abbaas (radhiyallahu 'anhuma) seated behind him, whilst Sayyiduna Usaamah (radhiyallahu 'anhu) was now walking.

In the days of Jaahiliyyah, the people would only leave Muzdalifah after sunrise. However, Rasulullah (sallallahu 'alaihi wasallam) opposed their practice and departed before sunrise. *(Saheeh Bukhaari #1684)*

Batnu Muhassir

When Rasulullah (sallallahu 'alaihi wasallam) reached Batnu Muhassir, which is a place between Mina and Muzdalifah, he urged the camel to move slightly faster. *(Saheeh Muslim #2950)*

The reason for this was that this was a place in which the punishment of Allah Ta'ala had descended in the past. Either, Abrahah and his army, who had come with the evil intention of demolishing the Ka'bah Shareef, had been destroyed here, or a

person who had violated the sanctity of the Haram by hunting in this place was divinely apprehended by a fire descending upon him. *(Mirqaat vol. 5, pg. 442)*

Although many years had passed since that time, Rasulullah (sallallahu 'alaihi wasallam) did not wish to be in a place that witnessed the punishment of Allah Ta'ala.[10]

We need to take a lesson from this and exercise great caution in this regard, by totally avoiding places of punishment (e.g. the Dead Sea), as well as places of sin and vice, since they are factors that speedily attract the wrath and punishment of Allah Ta'ala.

Another possible reason for Rasulullah (sallallahu 'alaihi wasallam) hastening through Batnu Muhassir is that the Christians would make wuqoof here. Hence, Rasulullah (sallallahu 'alaihi wasallam) wished to oppose them. *(Mirqaat vol. 5, pg. 442)*

---

[10] Similarly, on the way to Tabuk, when Rasulullah (sallallahu 'alaihi wasallam) passed by Hijr, the ruins of Thamood, he instructed the Sahaabah (radiyallahu 'anhum) to move on quickly and said to them: "Do not enter the dwellings of those who have oppressed themselves except in the condition that you cry, out of the fear that the same punishment may afflict you." He (sallallahu 'alaihi wasallam) also prohibited them from drinking or drawing water from it's well. The Sahaabah (radiyallahu 'anhum) said, "We have already pulled out water and made our dough (using this water)." Rasulullah (sallallahu 'alaihi wasallam) commanded them to dispose of the dough and throw away the water. Thereafter Rasulullah (sallallahu 'alaihi wasallam) covered himself with his shawl and rode his horse swiftly until he passed through and left the area. *(Saheeh Bukhaari #3378 & #3380 and Bazzaar - Majma'uz Zawaa-id #10377)*

Pelting

When travelling from Muzdalifah to Mina, Rasulullah (sallallahu 'alaihi wasallam) used the middle road, which leads directly to the Jamaratul 'Aqabah (the big 'Shaitaan').

When he reached there after sunrise, he faced the jamarah with the Ka'bah Shareef to his left and Mina to his right and pelted it with seven pebbles while seated on his camel. Rasulullah (sallallahu 'alaihi wasallam) only ceased to recite the talbiyah now, before pelting. He (sallallahu 'alaihi wasallam) threw the pebbles one-by-one and recited takbeer with every pebble.

Sayyiduna Bilaal (radhiyallahu 'anhu) was holding the reins of the camel of Rasulullah (sallallahu 'alaihi wasallam), while Sayyiduna Usaamah bin Zaid (radhiyallahu 'anhuma) was shading him from the sun with a cloth. Sayyiduna Fadhl (radhiyallahu 'anhu) was seated on the camel, behind Rasulullah (sallallahu 'alaihi wasallam), shielding him from any stones that may come towards him by mistake.

Farewell Hajj

Whilst pelting, mounted on his conveyance, Rasulullah (sallallahu 'alaihi wasallam) addressed the Sahaabah (radhiyallahu 'anhum) saying,

« لِتَأْخُذُوْا مَنَاسِكَكُمْ ، فَإِنِّيْ لَا أَدْرِيْ لَعَلِّيْ لَا أَحُجُّ بَعْدَ حَجَّتِيْ هٰذِهِ »

> *"Learn the rites of hajj, for I do not know perhaps I will not perform hajj after this hajj of mine." (Saheeh Muslim #3137)*

In this statement, Rasulullah (sallallahu 'alaihi wasallam) actually bade the Ummah farewell and indicated to them that his demise was imminent. Therefore, this hajj became known as "The Farewell Hajj". Furthermore, he encouraged them to take advantage of the opportunity which they had, and to thus learn from him the matters of Deen. *(Sharhun Nawawi)*

Farewell Khutbah

After pelting the Jamaratul 'Aqabah, Rasulullah (sallallahu 'alaihi wasallam) delivered a khutbah in which he gave pertinent parting advice to the Ummah at large.

Sayyiduna 'Ali (radhiyallahu 'anhu) was conveying the words of Rasulullah (sallallahu 'alaihi wasallam) to those who were far and thus unable to hear him directly.

Sayyiduna Abu Bakrah (radhiyallahu 'anhu) reports that Rasulullah (sallallahu 'alaihi wasallam) addressed the Sahaabah (radhiyallahu 'anhum) on the Day of Nahr (10th Zul Hijjah) and said,

Time has Rotated

« إِنَّ الزَّمَانَ قَدِ اسْتَدَارَ كَهَيْئَتِهِ يَوْمَ خَلَقَ اللهُ السَّمَوَاتِ وَالْأَرْضَ ، اَلسَّنَةُ اثْنَا عَشَرَ شَهْرًا ، مِنْهَا أَرْبَعَةٌ حُرُمٌ ، ثَلَاثٌ مُتَوَالِيَاتٌ : ذُو الْقَعْدَةِ وَذُو الْحِجَّةِ وَالْمُحَرَّمُ وَرَجَبُ مُضَرَ الَّذِيْ بَيْنَ جُمَادَى وَشَعْبَانَ »

> "Indeed time has rotated (until the months have now returned to their original sequence) as it was on the day that Allah Ta'ala created the heavens and the earth. The year consists of twelve months, of which four are sacred. Three of them are consecutive i.e. Zul Qa'dah, Zul Hijjah and Muharram, and Rajab of Mudhar which is between Jumaadal (Ukhraa) and Sha'baan."

All the Ambiyaa ('alaihimus salaam) would honour the four sacred months. The Arabs, who claimed to follow Nabi Ebrahim ('alaihis salaam), also understood and acknowledged the sanctity of these four months. However, they were a people who fought and waged war almost all-year round. Hence observing the sanctity of these months by abstaining from fighting was inconvenient for them. Therefore, they would manipulate these months by switching them around for their convenience.[11]

Because of this taking place excessively, the months of the year were mixed up to such an extent that at times, the month which they declared as Zul Hijjah was not really Zul Hijjah due to their switching. However, in the year in which Rasulullah (sallallahu 'alaihi wasallam) performed hajj, the months had returned to their original places. *(Ma'aariful Quraan vol. 4, vol. 370)*

---

[11] The lesson understood here is that we cannot make adjustments in Deen to suit our convenience. Rather, we should adjust ourselves to suit Deen. The Quraan Majeed repeatedly reprimands the Jews for making changes in Deen to suit themselves. Unfortunately, this is becoming very common nowadays.

Sanctity of a Muslim

Rasulullah (sallallahu 'alaihi wasallam) then asked the Sahaabah (radhiyallahu 'anhum),

« أَيُّ شَهْرٍ هٰذَا ؟ »

"Which month is this?"

Due to their high level of respect for Rasulullah (sallallahu 'alaihi wasallam), the Sahaabah (radhiyallahu 'anhum) replied, "Allah and His Rasul (sallallahu 'alaihi wasallam) know best." On this, Rasulullah (sallallahu 'alaihi wasallam) remained silent until they felt that he was going to give it another name. He then said,

« أَلَيْسَ ذَا الْحِجَّةِ ؟ »

"Is it not (the month of) Zul Hijjah?"

When they replied in the affirmative, he next asked,

« أَيُّ بَلَدٍ هٰذَا ؟ »

"Which place is this?"

Again, out of respect, the Sahaabah (radhiyallahu 'anhum) replied, "Allah and His Rasul (sallallahu 'alaihi wasallam) know best." Rasulullah (sallallahu 'alaihi wasallam) remained silent until they felt that he was going to give it another name. He then asked,

« أَلَيْسَ الْبَلْدَةَ ؟ »

"Is it not the (sacred) city?"

When they again replied in the affirmative, he asked,

« فَأَيُّ يَوْمٍ هٰذَا ؟ »

"Then, which day is this?"

Once more, they replied, "Allah and His Rasul (sallallahu 'alaihi wasallam) know best." Rasulullah (sallallahu 'alaihi wasallam) again remained silent until they felt that he was going to give it another name. He then asked,

« أَلَيْسَ يَوْمَ النَّحْرِ ؟ »

"Is it not the Day of Nahr (10th Zul Hijjah)?"

When the Sahaabah (radhiyallahu 'anhum) replied positively, Rasulullah (sallallahu 'alaihi wasallam) finally said,

« فَإِنَّ دِمَاءَكُمْ وَأَمْوَالَكُمْ وَأَعْرَاضَكُمْ عَلَيْكُمْ حَرَامٌ كَحُرْمَةِ يَوْمِكُمْ هٰذَا فِيْ بَلَدِكُمْ هٰذَا فِيْ شَهْرِكُمْ هٰذَا »

"Indeed, your blood, wealth and honour are sacred (i.e. haraam for another person to violate) upon you, just like the sanctity of this day of yours, in this place of yours, in this month of yours."

As explained earlier, despite the occasion enjoying three levels of sanctity, the sanctity of a Muslim was still shown to be greater. It is so unfortunate that today, we look for every opportunity to do a Muslim down. Further, his honour has become so cheap that based on mere suspicions, we blacken his name and tarnish his reputation, broadcasting all sorts of lies regarding him, especially via social media.

Although Rasulullah (sallallahu 'alaihi wasallam) mentioned this advice the day before in his khutbah in 'Arafaat, he repeated it in Mina as well, due to the importance of this aspect. *(Jaami'ul 'Uloomi wal Hikam pg. 433)*

Meeting Allah Ta'ala

« وَسَتَلْقَوْنَ رَبَّكُمْ فَيَسْأَلُكُمْ عَنْ أَعْمَالِكُمْ »

"Soon you will meet your Rabb, and He will question you regarding your actions."

Meeting Allah Ta'ala and giving an account of our deeds is a belief which every true believer possesses. However, the need is for one to constantly be concious of it, as it is this belief which will set many of his issues straight.

Internal Fighting

« أَلاَ فَلاَ تَرْجِعُوا بَعْدِيْ ضُلَّالًا، يَضْرِبُ بَعْضُكُمْ رِقَابَ بَعْضٍ »

"Listen! Do not return to misguidance after me, (by) some of you striking the necks of others."

Passing the Message

« فَلْيُبَلِّغِ الشَّاهِدُ الْغَائِبَ ، فَرُبَّ مُبَلَّغٍ أَوْعَى مِنْ سَامِعٍ » .

"The one who is present should convey the message to those who are absent, as many of those to whom the message is conveyed preserve the message better than those who hear the message (directly)." (Saheeh Bukhaari #1741 & # 5550)

Rasulullah (sallallahu 'alaihi wasallam) was perpetually filled with a deep concern for his Ummah. As the followers and ardent lovers of Rasulullah (sallallahu 'alaihi wasallam), we should also have a concern for the Ummah and those around us.

Hence, beginning with our children, immediate family and friends, each person should make an effort to pass on the message of Deen and imaan and improve the Islamic condition of each person, including himself.

Importance of Segregation

After delivering the khutbah, various people came forward to present their questions to Rasulullah (sallallahu 'alaihi wasallam).

At that time, a young, attractive girl from the tribe of Khath'am came to Rasulullah (sallallahu 'alaihi wasallam) to ask him regarding her father, as he was unable to sit on a conveyance and thus could not perform hajj. Rasulullah (sallallahu 'alaihi wasallam) instructed her to perform hajj on his behalf.

While the young girl was posing her question, Sayyiduna Fadhl (radhiyallahu 'anhu) happened to look towards her. Rasulullah (sallallahu 'alaihi wasallam) immediately held his chin and turned his face away.

When Sayyiduna 'Abbaas (radhiyallahu 'anhu) asked him the reason for this, he said,

« رَأَيْتُ شَابًّا وَشَابَّةً فَلَمْ آمَنْ الشَّيْطَانَ عَلَيْهِمَا »

"I saw a young man and a young woman, so I did not feel safe of Shaitaan (exerting his influence) over them (and involving them in sin)." (Saheeh Bukhaari #4399 & Sunan Tirmizi #885)

These were Sahaabah (radhiyallahu 'anhum), and they were in the most sacred of places, carrying out the great 'ibaadah of hajj, in the most blessed company of Rasulullah (sallallahu 'alaihi wasallam). However, Rasulullah (sallallahu 'alaihi wasallam) ensured that the laws of men not looking at women were upheld.

Thus, for us to be lax with regards to the laws of segregation and purdah, and then justify it by saying that 'our hearts are clean', is an indirect accusation against these Sahaabah (radhiyallahu 'anhum) – by insinuating that they needed to lower their gazes because their hearts were dirty (Allah Ta'ala forbid!)

Allocating Places

Rasulullah (sallallahu 'alaihi wasallam) then showed the Sahaabah (radhiyallahu 'anhum) where they should encamp. He told the Muhaajireen (radhiyallahu 'anhum) to encamp at the front right section of Masjid Khaif (the masjid in Mina), the Ansaar (radhiyallahu 'anhum) at the back left section of the masjid, and the other Sahaabah (radhiyallahu 'anhum) around them.

Slaughtering the Camels

Rasulullah (sallallahu 'alaihi wasallam) then proceeded to slaughter his sacrificial animals. His place of slaughter was in front of the masjid, where he (sallallahu 'alaihi wasallam) was encamped.

Rasulullah (sallallahu 'alaihi wasallam) slaughtered sixty-three camels with his own blessed hands. These were the camels that he had brought with him from Madeenah Munawwarah. Sayyiduna 'Ali (radhiyallahu 'anhu) slaughtered the remainder of the camels (thirty-seven) on his own. These were the camels that he had brought from Yemen.

Rasulullah (sallallahu 'alaihi wasallam) also slaughtered animals on behalf of his respected wives.

Whilst slaughtering the camels, five or six of the camels rushed towards Rasulullah (sallallahu 'alaihi wasallam), as each wished to have the honour of being slaughtered by his blessed hand first. *(Sunan Abi Dawood #1765)*

Subhaanallah! Even animals were brimming with such love for Rasulullah (sallallahu 'alaihi wasallam) that they were eager to sacrifice their lives in order to earn the honour of being slaughtered at the blessed hand of Rasulullah (sallallahu 'alaihi wasallam).[12]

---

[12] If we claim to have love for Rasulullah (sallallahu 'alaihi wasallam), then the very least that we can do is sacrifice our desires in order to revive the sunnah of Rasulullah (sallallahu 'alaihi wasallam) and live our lives according to his Deen. The next time we are tempted to abandon the sunnah of Rasulullah (sallallahu 'alaihi wasallam), let us place the knife of the sunnah on the neck of our desires and spill the blood of true love.

Partaking of the Meat

Rasulullah (sallallahu 'alaihi wasallam) then instructed that a piece of meat from every one of the hundred camels be placed into a pot and cooked together. Rasulullah (sallallahu 'alaihi wasallam) and Sayyiduna 'Ali (radhiyallahu 'anhu) then ate from the meat and sipped the gravy. *(Saheeh Muslim #2950)*

Rasulullah (sallallahu 'alaihi wasallam) wished to honour the invitation of Allah Ta'ala and gain the tremendous blessings contained in the meat of the animals – but how could he eat from a hundred camels?

In order to do so, a piece of meat from every camel was placed into a pot and it was all cooked together. Thereafter, when Rasulullah (sallallahu 'alaihi wasallam) ate from the pot and drank from the gravy, he secured, in just a few morsels, the blessings of one hundred camels. *(Sharhun Nawawi)*

Blessed Hair

After slaughtering, Rasulullah (sallallahu 'alaihi wasallam) called Sayyiduna Ma'mar bin 'Abdillah (radhiyallahu 'anhu) to shave his blessed head. He instructed him to shave the right side first and then the left.

Rasulullah (sallallahu 'alaihi wasallam) also trimmed his blessed nails, shortened his blessed moustache and trimmed his blessed beard.

Rasulullah (sallallahu 'alaihi wasallam) gave half his hair to Sayyiduna Abu Talhah and his wife, Sayyidah Ummu Sulaim (radhiyallahu 'anhuma), and instructed Sayyiduna Abu Talhah (radhiyallahu 'anhu) to distribute the other half between the Sahaabah (radhiyallahu 'anhum).

The Sahaabah (radhiyallahu 'anhum) would thereafter derive barakah (blessings) from the blessed hair of Rasulullah (sallallahu 'alaihi wasallam).

Similarly, the blessed nails of Rasulullah (sallallahu 'alaihi wasallam) were also distributed among the Sahaabah (radhiyallahu 'anhum).

Hence, before Sayyiduna Mu'aawiyah (radhiyallahu 'anhu) passed away, He bequeathed that the nail clippings of Rasulullah (sallallahu 'alaihi wasallam), which were in his possession, be filed down to powder form and placed in his eyes and mouth. (Usdul Ghaabah vol. 4, pg. 156)

Rasulullah (sallallahu 'alaihi wasallam) made du'aa thrice for Allah Ta'ala to forgive those men who shaved their heads, and once for those who merely trimmed their hair, indicating that shaving is more virtuous and rewarding than trimming the hair. (Saheeh Bukhaari #1728 and Sharhuz Zurqaani vol. 11, pg. 439)

Going to Makkah Mukarramah

Rasulullah (sallallahu 'alaihi wasallam) then wore normal clothing and applied 'itr. He departed for Makkah Mukarramah before Zuhr Salaah, riding his camel.

After performing Tawaafuz Ziyaarah, Rasulullah (sallallahu 'alaihi wasallam) went to the well of Zamzam where his family members were drawing the water and serving the people, as this was their responsibility

Due to the great virtue of this act, Rasulullah (sallallahu 'alaihi wasallam) wished to personally assist in drawing the water, but did not do so saying,

« اِنْزِعُوْا بَنِيْ عَبْدِ الْمُطَّلِبِ ! فَلَوْلَا أَنْ يَغْلِبَكُمُ النَّاسُ عَلَى سِقَايَتِكُمْ لَنَزَعْتُ مَعَكُمْ »

"Draw! O children of 'Abdul Muttalib! If it was not for the (fear of) people overwhelming you in your drawing the water, I would also draw (Zamzam) with you."

Had the people seen Rasulullah (sallallahu 'alaihi wasallam) drawing water, they would have understood it to be one of the rites of hajj and would have thus all flocked to the well to draw water. Naturally, this would have caused great inconvenience on account of the space being restricted and it would also result in the Banu 'Abdil Muttalib being deprived of carrying out this great service and virtuous deed.

Thereafter, they offered Zamzam to Rasulullah (sallallahu 'alaihi wasallam) and he drank it while standing. *(Saheeh Muslim #2950 and Sharhun Nawawi)*

Rasulullah (sallallahu 'alaihi wasallam) thereafter performed sa'ee, after which he (sallallahu 'alaihi wasallam) performed Zuhr Salaah, either in Makkah Mukarramah or after returning to Mina, and spent that night and the following two nights in Mina.

Remaining Days

Pelting

The next day (11ᵗʰ Zul Hijjah), after zawaal, Rasulullah (sallallahu 'alaihi wasallam) walked to the Jamaraat and began pelting from the first Jamarah. After pelting it with seven stones, reciting takbeer with every stone, he engaged in du'aa for the duration of time that it takes to recite Surah Baqarah. He (sallallahu 'alaihi wasallam) thereafter pelted the second and again engaged in a lengthy du'aa. After pelting the third, he (sallallahu 'alaihi wasallam) did not engage in any du'aa.

Rasulullah (sallallahu 'alaihi wasallam) did the same on the 12ᵗʰ of Zul Hijjah (5ᵗʰ day of hajj) as well.

During these nights in Mina, Rasulullah (sallallahu 'alaihi wasallam) would go to Makkah Mukarramah to perform tawaaf.

Surah Nasr

Sayyiduna 'Abdullah bin 'Umar (radhiyallahu 'anhuma) narrates that Surah Nasr was revealed in Mina in the middle day of the

days of tashreeq (i.e. 11th Zul Hijjah). *(As-Sunanul Kubraa – Baihaqi #9682)*

Rasulullah (sallallahu 'alaihi wasallam) understood from this surah that the time of his demise had drawn near. Sayyiduna 'Abdullah bin 'Abbaas (radhiyallahu 'anhuma) reports that when Surah Nasr was revealed, Rasulullah (sallallahu 'alaihi wasallam) mentioned that his demise would transpire that very year saying, "I have been informed of my (imminent) demise." *(Musnad Ahmad #1873)*

Khutbah

Rasulullah (sallallahu 'alaihi wasallam) delivered a khutbah on 11th Zul Hijjah as well.

Once again in this khutbah, Rasulullah (sallallahu 'alaihi wasallam) explained the sanctity of the blood, wealth and honour of a Muslim, as he had explained in the previous two days. *(Jaami'ul 'Uloomi wal Hikam pg. 433)*

Thereafter, Rasulullah (sallallahu 'alaihi wasallam) said,

Oppression and Extortion

« اِسْمَعُوْا مِنِّيْ تَعِيْشُوْا ، أَلَا لَا تَظْلِمُوْا ، أَلَا لَا تَظْلِمُوْا ، أَلَا لَا تَظْلِمُوْا ، إِنَّهُ لَا يَحِلُّ مَالُ امْرِئٍ مُسْلِمٍ إِلَّا بِطِيْبِ نَفْسٍ مِنْهُ »

"Listen to me, you will live (a good life). Behold! Do not oppress! Behold! Do not oppress! Behold! Do not oppress! The wealth of a Muslim is not permissible except with his happiness." *(Musnad Ahmad #20695)*

Oppression is such a heinous crime that Rasulullah (sallallahu 'alaihi wasallam) repeated its prohibition thrice. Although there are various ways in which oppression happens, Rasulullah (sallallahu 'alaihi wasallam) focused on the aspect of oppressing people by extortion (extracting money from people against their will).

There are many different forms of extortion. One form of extortion occurs in the winding up of the deceased's estate. One or more of the heirs deliberately set out to deprive other heirs – primarily the women – of the fair share which sharee'ah has stipulated for them.

Another form of extortion is where a person is in financial constraints and thus resorts to selling some of his assets in desperation. Knowing fully well that the person is in a 'squeeze', we happily squeeze him further by offering him an amount that we know is below the value of the asset. Eventually, the person accepts, as he is desperate for the cash. However, such a transaction, although valid, will never carry barakah (blessings) as the seller agreed with an unhappy heart.[13]

---

[13] There are also other more subtle, sophisticated and polished manners of extortion which have even become socially acceptable. A few examples of these forms of extortion are bridal showers, baby showers and housewarming parties. For these occasions, the guests are expected to arrive with a gift in hand. Hence, those invited feel compelled to present the host with a gift – even if it is difficult for them to manage – as arriving empty-handed will be a source of embarrassment and disgrace.

One very common problem which also falls under extortion is where an employer exploits his employee and takes advantage of his plight by forcing him to work overtime, etc. without remunerating him correctly.

Internal Fighting

« أَلَا إِنَّ الشَّيْطَانَ قَدْ أَيِسَ أَنْ يَعْبُدَهُ الْمُصَلُّونَ ، وَلَكِنْ فِي التَّحْرِيْشِ بَيْنَكُمْ »

"Listen! Shaitaan has lost hope that the people of salaah (i.e. the Muslims) will worship him, however (he has hope) in creating discord among you." (Musnad Ahmad #20695)

In this advice, Rasulullah (sallallahu 'alaihi wasallam) warned the Ummah that Shaitaan's plot and plan is to create discord, dissension and disunity among the Ummah. At times, the disunity will be among, families, at times it will be among communities, and at times, it will be among the Muslims in general.[14]

One of the reasons why Shaitaan strives to create disunity between people is that once disunity is created, it opens the

---

[14] It should be borne in mind that in Islam, the only unity that is sought is unity upon the truth. Hence, if one party is calling the other to unite with them by compromising on Deeni values (e.g. attending a mixed function), then one should not unite with them but should rather remain firm upon Deen. In such a case, uniting with them, in reality, will be to unite upon sin.
On the contrary, if the dispute does not involve the laws of Deen and the sharee'ah, but is rather a dispute relating to people's personal rights (e.g. a monetary dispute), then in this case, viewing the broader interest of unity, if one is happy to reach a compromise by foregoing his right, then one will be greatly rewarded by Allah Ta'ala.

floodgates of other sins. In the wake of disunity follow sins of harbouring enmity in the heart, making gheebah (backbiting), carrying tales, slandering and other similar evils. Thus, disunity is a lucrative "investment" for Shaitaan – one which we must try our best to avoid.

Racism

« يَا أَيُّهَا النَّاسُ ! أَلَا إِنَّ رَبَّكُمْ وَاحِدٌ وَإِنَّ أَبَاكُمْ وَاحِدٌ ، أَلَا لَا فَضْلَ لِعَرَبِيٍّ عَلَى عَجَمِيٍّ وَلَا لِعَجَمِيٍّ عَلَى عَرَبِيٍّ ، وَلَا أَحْمَرَ عَلَى أَسْوَدَ وَلَا أَسْوَدَ عَلَى أَحْمَرَ إِلَّا بِالتَّقْوَى »

"O people! Indeed, your Rabb is One, and your father (i.e. Nabi Aadam ['alaihis salaam]) is one. Listen! No Arab holds virtue over a non-Arab, and no non-Arab has virtue over an Arab (due to nationality). No black person has virtue over a white person, and no white person has virtue over a black person (due to the colour of their skin) – except through taqwa (i.e. it is only one's taqwa that will cause one to be more virtuous in the sight of Allah Ta'ala). (Musnad Ahmad #23489)

In the Quraan Majeed, Allah Ta'ala states,

يَٰٓأَيُّهَا النَّاسُ إِنَّا خَلَقْنَٰكُم مِّن ذَكَرٍ وَأُنثَىٰ وَجَعَلْنَٰكُمْ شُعُوبًا وَقَبَآئِلَ لِتَعَارَفُوٓا۟ ۚ إِنَّ أَكْرَمَكُمْ عِندَ ٱللَّهِ أَتْقَىٰكُمْ

"O people! Indeed, We have created you from one man and one woman (i.e. Nabi Aadam and Sayyidah Hawwaa ['alaihimas salaam], and We made you into nations and tribes so that you may know (and distinguish between) one another. Indeed, the most honourable of you in the sight of Allah Ta'ala is the one who possesses the most taqwa."
(Surah Hujuraat v13)

In the abovementioned hadeeth and verse of the Quraan Majeed, we are taught that the basis for a Muslim having honour in the sight of Allah Ta'ala is taqwa – the awareness and consciousness of Allah Ta'ala. Therefore, it is not the colour of our skins that will determine our position in the Hereafter – it is our actions. Hence, we should never despise the next person due to their race, nationality or the colour of their skin.

Sayyiduna Bilaal (radhiyallahu 'anhu) was a dark-skinned, former slave from Africa. Yet, due to his imaan and taqwa, Rasulullah (sallallahu 'alaihi wasallam) held him in such esteem that he made him his treasurer, appointed him as the first muazzin in Islam and testified that he had heard his footsteps in Jannah.

Fulfilling the Trust

« يَا أَيُّهَا النَّاسُ ! مَنْ كَانَتْ عِنْدَهُ وَدِيعَةٌ فَلْيُؤَدِّهَا إِلَى مَنِ ائْتَمَنَهُ عَلَيْهَا »

"O people! Whoever has a trust with him, he should fulfil it (by returning it) to the one who entrusted it to him." (Bazzaar - Majm'uz Zawaaid #5687)

The quality of trustworthiness and honesty is a basic and salient feature of a Muslim, so much so that the lack of this quality has been declared as being one of the distinct features of a hypocrite.

Such was the trustworthiness of Rasulullah (sallallahu 'alaihi wasallam) that even before nubuwwah, the disbelievers of Makkah Mukarramah would leave their valuables with him for safekeeping. After nubuwwah as well, even though the disbelievers opposed Islam and were his enemies, on account of his unparalleled trustworthiness, they still entrusted him with their wealth for safekeeping.

Insignificant Sins

« أَيُّهَا النَّاسُ ! إِنَّ الشَّيْطَانَ قَدْ أَيِسَ أَنْ يُعْبَدَ بِبِلَادِكُمْ آخِرَ الزَّمَانِ ، وَقَدْ رَضِيَ مِنْكُمْ بِمُحَقَّرَاتِ الْأَعْمَالِ ، فَاحْذَرُوا عَلَى دِيْنِكُمْ مُحَقَّرَاتِ الْأَعْمَالِ »

"O people! Indeed, Shaitaan has lost all hope of him being worshipped in your land until the end of time, however he is pleased with you falling into (wrong) actions which are regarded as insignificant. Therefore, in regard to your Deen, beware of the (wrong) actions which are considered insignificant." (Bazzaar – Majm'uz Zawaaid #5687)

When we view this advice of Rasulullah (sallallahu 'alaihi wasallam), then we find that there are many sins which people regard to be insignificant. People carry out these sins casually, without feeling any remorse or reluctance, and feel that what they have done is nothing serious.

In this regard, we must not look at the sin and consider it small – we must look at the One whose law is being broken and who is being disobeyed. We must look at His greatness, and then we will realize the seriousness of the sin.

One reason why these types of sins are so destructive, due to which Shaitaan tries to make people fall into them, is that due to people considering them insignificant, they do not make taubah for them.

Secondly, these sins are carried out repeatedly, with a sense of impunity. Due to being repeated over and over, they cause a person to fall deep into sin.

Thirdly, by one regarding the sins to be insignificant, he shows disregard to the sanctity of the sharee'ah and the importance of Allah Ta'ala's laws. This is a serious and major sin in itself.

Therefore, we must never regard any sin to be small and insignificant, but must repent for every sin and try to abstain from every evil.

True Muslim, Mu-min, Muhaajir and Mujaahid

« وَسَأُخْبِرُكُمْ مَنِ الْمُسْلِمِ، الْمُسْلِمُ مَنْ سَلِمَ النَّاسُ مِنْ لِسَانِهِ وَيَدِهِ، وَالْمُؤْمِنُ مَنْ أَمِنَهُ النَّاسُ عَلَى أَمْوَالِهِمْ وَأَنْفُسِهِمْ، وَالْمُهَاجِرُ مَنْ هَجَرَ الْخَطَايَا وَالذُّنُوبَ، وَالْمُجَاهِدُ مَنْ جَاهَدَ نَفْسَهُ فِي طَاعَةِ اللهِ. »

"I will inform you as to who a true Muslim is. A true Muslim is the one from whose hand and tongue people are safe, and a true believer is he from whom the people are safe in regard to their wealth and lives, and a true muhaajir (one who migrates) is the one who abandons sins, and a true mujaahid is the one who strives to obey Allah Ta'ala against his desires." (Bazzaar - Majm'uz Zawaaid #5690)[15]

A true Muslim and a true believer is a person who does not cause any harm, pain or anguish, whether mental, physical, financial

---

[15] NB: Contrary to the narrations regarding the other advices, this narration does not specifically mention the time in which this was mentioned by Rasulullah (sallallahu 'alaihi wasallam) during his hajj.

or emotional, to another person. Rasulullah (sallallahu 'alaihi wasallam) showed this to be a quality that is linked to a person's imaan and Islam (i.e. without a person possessing this quality, his Islam and imaan are deficient).

Although a muhaajir refers to a person who gives up his home town and migrates to another place for the sake of Allah Ta'ala and his Deen, Rasulullah (sallallahu 'alaihi wasallam) explained that a true muhaajir is the one who gives up and abandons sins.

Rasulullah (sallallahu 'alaihi wasallam) further mentioned that the true mujaahid is the one who 'wages war' against his desires and strives to obey Allah Ta'ala.

The reason for the person engaging in this form of jihaad (i.e. jihaad against the carnal self) being called a true mujaahid is that this form of jihaad is a perpetual jihaad, as opposed to a battle which lasts for a few moments. In battle, a person either wins, gaining booty and reward, or is killed, gaining martyrdom and reward. However, in jihaad against one's carnal desires, the person only wins when he dies with imaan and only sees his rewards in the Hereafter.

Departure from Mina

Rasulullah (sallallahu 'alaihi wasallam) remained in Mina until he had pelted on the 13th as well. Thereafter he departed after zawaal.

Muhassab

Sayyiduna Abu Raafi' (radhiyallahu 'anhu), the freed slave of Rasulullah (sallallahu 'alaihi wasallam), whose name was Aslam, erected a tent of hide for Rasulullah (sallallahu 'alaihi wasallam) at a place called Muhassab.[16] He was in charge of the luggage of Rasulullah (sallallahu 'alaihi wasallam).

Rasulullah (sallallahu 'alaihi wasallam) thus camped here and performed four salaah here i.e. Zuhr until 'Esha.

Final Tawaaf and Fajr

At the time of sehri, Rasulullah (sallallahu 'alaihi wasallam) went to Makkah Mukarramah and performed Tawaaful Wadaa'. Rasulullah (sallallahu 'alaihi wasallam) performed Fajr Salaah in Makkah Mukarramah and recited Surah Toor during the salaah.

'Umrah of Aaishah (radhiyallahu 'anha)

That same night, Rasulullah (sallallahu 'alaihi wasallam) sent Sayyidah 'Aaishah (radhiyallahu 'anha) with her brother, Sayyiduna 'Abdur Rahmaan bin Abi Bakr (radhiyallahu 'anhuma), to perform 'umrah from Tan'eem.

---

[16] This place is also known as Hasbaa, Abtah, Bat-haa, and Khaifu Bani Kinaanah.

This 'umrah was qadhaa of the 'umrah that was cancelled when she experienced her monthly cycle.

Rasulullah (sallallahu 'alaihi wasallam) waited for her in Muhassab. When she had completed her 'umrah, Rasulullah (sallallahu 'alaihi wasallam) gave the instruction for departure.

لَبَّيْكَ اَللّٰهُمَّ لَبَّيْكَ ، لَبَّيْكَ لَا شَرِيْكَ لَكَ لَبَّيْكَ ، إِنَّ الْحَمْدَ وَالنِّعْمَةَ لَكَ وَالْمُلْكَ ، لَا شَرِيْكَ لَكَ

Return

Departure

Rasulullah (sallallahu 'alaihi wasallam) then left Makkah Mukarramah from the path of Kudaa. He (sallallahu 'alaihi wasallam) took some Zamzam along with him.

The departure of Rasulullah (sallallahu 'alaihi wasallam) was on the morning of Wednesday 14th Zul Hijjah.

Ghadeeru Khum

When Rasulullah (sallallahu 'alaihi wasallam) reached Ghadeeru Khum on Sunday 18th Zul Hijjah, he delivered a khutbah in which he praised Sayyiduna 'Ali (radhiyallahu 'anhu). This was to clarify the innocence of Sayyiduna 'Ali (radhiyallahu 'anhu) regarding the accusations that had been levelled against him in Yemen. *(Al-Bidaayah wan Nihaayah vol. 5, pg. 309)*

Night in Zul Hulaifah

When Rasulullah (sallallahu 'alaihi wasallam) reached Zul Hulaifah, he spent the night there, and entered Madeenah Munawwarah the next day from the road of Mu'arras.

Uhud

As the mountain of Uhud appeared before Rasulullah (sallallahu 'alaihi wasallam), he said,

« هٰذَا جَبَلٌ يُحِبُّنَا وَنُحِبُّهُ »

"This is a mountain that loves us and we love it." (Saheeh Bukhaari #4084 and Fathul Baari)

The du'aa which we could make is that when Allah Ta'ala blessed a hard mountain with the love of Rasulullah (sallallahu 'alaihi wasallam), He should also fill our hard hearts with this love.

Du'aa

When Rasulullah's (sallallahu 'alaihi wasallam) blessed gaze fell on Madeenah Munawwarah, he said "Allahu Akbar" thrice and then recited,

« لَا إِلٰهَ إِلَّا اللهُ وَحْدَهُ لَا شَرِيْكَ لَهُ لَهُ الْمُلْكُ وَلَهُ الْحَمْدُ وَهُوَ عَلٰى كُلِّ شَيْءٍ قَدِيْرٌ ، آئِبُوْنَ تَائِبُوْنَ عَابِدُوْنَ سَاجِدُوْنَ لِرَبِّنَا حَامِدُوْنَ ، صَدَقَ اللهُ وَعْدَهُ وَنَصَرَ عَبْدَهُ وَهَزَمَ الْأَحْزَابَ وَحْدَهُ »

"There is none worthy of worship besides Allah Ta'ala, who is alone and has no partner. To Him alone belongs the kingdom, and to Him alone belongs all praise, and He has complete power over everything. (We are) returning while repenting, worshipping, prostrating to our Rabb and

praising (Allah Ta'ala). Allah Ta'ala fulfilled His promise, and assisted His slave, and He alone defeated the groups (and armies of the disbelievers)." (Sharhuz Zurqaani vol. 11, pg. 475)

Like Hajj with Me

Sayyidah Ummu Sinaan and Sayyidah Ummu Ma'qil (radhiyallahu 'anhuma) were unable to perform hajj with Rasulullah (sallallahu 'alaihi wasallam) due to some valid reasons.

On his return from hajj, when Rasulullah (sallallahu 'alaihi wasallam) met them, he (sallallahu 'alaihi wasallam) informed them that performing 'umrah during the month of Ramadhaan would earn a person the reward of hajj or hajj performed with Rasulullah (sallallahu 'alaihi wasallam). *(Saheeh Bukhaari #1782 & #1863, Sunan Abi Dawood #1989 and Fat-hul Baari)*

May Allah Ta'ala bless us with the blessings of the Farewell Hajj, grant us the ability to practice on the parting advice of our beloved Rasul (sallallahu 'alaihi wasallam) and bless us with true love for his esteemed self that is translated into following his pure and perfect way of life, aameen.

لَبَّيْكَ اللّٰهُمَّ لَبَّيْكَ ، لَبَّيْكَ لَا شَرِيْكَ لَكَ لَبَّيْكَ ، إِنَّ الْحَمْدَ وَالنِّعْمَةَ لَكَ وَالْمُلْكَ ، لَا شَرِيْكَ لَكَ

www.ingramcontent.com/pod-product-compliance
Lightning Source LLC
LaVergne TN
LVHW021053100526
838202LV00083B/5841